LIVE, LEARN, AND LOVE SMART

AUTHENTIC STORIES OF TRIALS AND TRIUMPHS, WITH AFFIRMATIONS TO FUEL YOUR SOUL

SANDYE LOMAX

13TH & JOAN

For permission requests, write to the publisher, addressed "Attention: Permissions Coordinator," 205 N. Michigan Avenue, Suite #810, Chicago, IL 60601. 13th & Joan books may be purchased for educational, business or sales promotional use. For information, please email the Sales Department at sales@13thandjoan.com.

Printed in the U. S. A.

First Printing, July 2025

Library of Congress Cataloging-in-Publication Data has been applied for.

ISBN: 978-1-961863-83-5

Dedication

This book is dedicated to my beautiful and amazing mother, Dolores T. Lomax, affectionately referred to as Penny; and to my late grandmother, Beulah Pinkney, aka Mum.

Acknowledgements

*L*ET ME START with saying, *"We did it Mommy!"* Thank you for believing in me and in all that I choose to do. Every goal I set forth, every dream I dream up, and every crazy idea I believe I can achieve is because you support me and tell me "YES YOU CAN!" You jump right in and dream alongside me to help bring them to life. I love you beyond any words I could ever type or say. I can't say thank you enough for leading me to God from the day I came out of your womb and for teaching me that I can do all things through Christ who loves and strengthens me. I appreciate you for consistently praying for me no matter the day or hour. You never tried to discourage me from trying new things. When I was younger, I once told you that a friend and I thought about doing a make-up line after we'd been playing in a make-up store for hours. The next day, you sent me a list of creative names we could call each eyeshadow. I still have that list along with every birthday card and recipe you've ever given me. While writing this book, you were the only person I shared the ingredients with, allowing you to give me feedback and title cover ideas.

Thank you momma bear for always being my biggest supporter and best friend. I love you endlessly! Every loving, kind, creative gene I have stems from my mom. We laugh about this, but this is my personal apology for all the drama I now know that I put you through as a young teenage girl trying to be in the "it crowd" in the midst of learning who I was and was meant to be. I became caught between being a city and county girl who wanted to hang out all night with my friends who were allowed to. We didn't have cell phones back then, so I can't imagine how worried you must have been when I was being ridiculously rebellious staying out past my curfew or at Rhythm Skate late nights with my friends working on our New Edition girl rap and singing group routine before getting on the mic by midnight. Let's talk about the time I ran away from home and went to hide down the street behind the bushes in front of my middle school #180 in Cherry Hill only to return a few hours later because I was hungry? My sassy mouth was always running and thinking I knew it all. Lawwwd knows I didn't know nothing on top of nothing about what transitioning into adulthood would really be like. Thank you for never giving up on your "Sandye baby." My life's goal is to continue to make you proud. I love everything about you and thank God for blessing me with such an amazing mother! *You Light Up My Life and You're the Wind Beneath My Wings!* Thanks for being the most amazing mom ever!

Thank you to my guardian angel above, my grandmother Mum. I hope you are smiling down from the heavens with pride in your heart. Thank you for teaching me at a young age that my voice is powerful and should be heard, to never be afraid of telling my truths with my head held high, never down and whispering. You and Mommy both taught me the strength of a woman is undeniable! My grandmother taught me to have very thick skin at a young age. I watched her wash dishes with her bare hands in scalding hot water. She taught me "mind over matter" and that scalding hot water would burn germs cold water couldn't. Catch that lesson, baby. So when I felt the heat from that straightening comb hot off the stove's flame, I didn't say a word while squinting down in the chair. She taught me through her walk that my voice and what I would experience in life would matter. I can hear you saying, *"Awwh shucks now, go head kid, that's my girl!"* I love you forever Mum, my guardian angel.

I'm so grateful for my entire village of supporters. Forever proud to be from my hometown Baltimore, Maryland. I also have mad love for Atlanta, Georgia and the tribe there that rocks with me hard. The love and unwavering support from everyone keeps me motivated. No matter how you have contributed to my growth, thank you!

I am forever grateful to all who have taught me, been kind to me, patient with me, listened to me, and shared laughter, pain, tears, and joy with me. If you have crossed my path, there was a reason for it. If I learned anything from you, good or bad, thank you.

For I know the plans I have for you, declares the Lord.
Plans to prosper you and not to harm you,
plans to give you hope and a future.
Jeremiah 29:11

Contents

Introduction

ECOMING AN AUTHOR is by far one of my greatest accomplishments. At the end of the day, I'm just a girl from Baltimore who believes she can BMORE!! This book literally took everything I had and didn't know I had in me. It is truly a labor of love that I birthed, and I am so proud of myself for crossing the finish line. I wanted to quit so many times because being vulnerable has its personal challenges, but I realize it is super powerful when you do so. It took years, tears, stop and go, but here we are. Every time I put it to the side, God put it back in front of me. Every time I got in a groove of writing, the devil came with distractions. So I say to anyone reading this, do whatever it is that you want to do in life and don't give up. Do it even when you feel scared and uncertain. Be patient with yourself and get it done. Write your vision down and no matter how long it takes, bring it to life. The closer you get to achieving any goal, distractions will arise.

That is how you know you are going in the right direction and getting closer to achieving your goal.

This book was one of my passion and purpose projects that I set out to complete. The Most High's timing is perfect, so I have no regrets. It took a lot of prayer and sometimes involved intense anxiety from having to reflect, relive, and sustain the courage to share pieces of certain experiences that weren't easy. I thank God for laying this book on my heart and for the unconditional love, grace, and mercy God has shown me throughout my life's journey. To God Be the Glory! I thank you God for all you have done for me and for the countless ways you continue to guide and protect me. There is none like you!

In this book, I share some of my personal experiences that I have lived through and learned from. When I decided to open up about my take on life and how I'm still learning to live it, it was in hopes that you will either be able to relate, be inspired, or have a shortcut into learning from the things I had to learn from both good and bad. A lot of my life experiences taught me firsthand how to "love smart," whether it be in my career choices, friendships, relationships, family, or even self. If we shared our experiences and what we learned from them, I believe most of us would be 10 steps ahead in life. I started to understand more about life and myself when I realized I had to learn to face my past traumas to heal, be present in my current moments, and intelligently embrace what is to come. That meant sitting still with God and allowing myself to become self-absorbed, sitting alone and becoming centered with myself and only God present. One might say that being "self-absorbed" sounds selfish. When we hear the word selfish, most times it is viewed in a negative light. I have learned that it is indeed ok to be selfish when it comes to self-love. In fact, it is more than ok. It is a necessity, and it is smart.

Many people spend most of their days pouring into others, whether it be through work or personal life. Taking time to solely and unapologetically focus on you is extremely important. It is ok to be preoccupied with your own wants and needs. It does not mean that you lack love or interest in others, but you simply acknowledge that you must put yourself first to become all that you are meant to be. You can't pour from an empty cup, which is something I learned the hard way.

I must say that I have had the opportunity to live an amazing life, full of bumps and bruises, but worth sharing. I have had some experiences that one can only dream of and some nightmares others would hate to have had to sleep through. When I sit back and take it all in, I wouldn't change a thing because it has beautifully molded me into a unique masterpiece formed by God. This book allows me to share hope and to inspire others from a personal and authentic place. Some say it takes about 21 days to create a new habit, which is why I reference each chapter as a day. I want this book to be a leisure read based on what day may resonate to you throughout your life's journey.

The one point I really want to expound on is self-care. Old habits are hard to break. I had gotten in a poor habit of neglecting myself. On the outside everything looked fine but on the inside, I was starving myself in ways I didn't even know. Wellness is a word we hear often these days. Practicing self-care is one of the smartest habits you can create. I now take whatever time is necessary to be still in silence and acknowledge the love and attention I'm pouring into myself. If you're like me, you know that sometimes taking one day off is not enough. By the time you start to feel rested, refreshed and/or re-energized, it's time to jump right back into life's hustle and bustle. You think to yourself, *"I wish I had just one more day"* or *"What about a few weeks off with pay to just LET GO?"* A return home from a weekend vacation never feels like it was long enough for me, but a breakaway is better than not having taken any time off. Makes sense when you do the math on how we tend to always seem to have an uneven work-life balance.

In this world today, we experience so much trauma that we can't unsee, unhear, or erase from our memories--from mass school shootings, pandemics, inflation, personal loss and sickness, etc. Things we used to only see in movies have become real-life scenes. Most times it's hard to find time to properly grieve, heal, and process life's experiences because life goes on during it all. Time is the one thing that does not stop, pause, or slow down. Because the clock keeps ticking forward, life will continue to happen as long as you're living. Trust me, there were many times I wanted to stop the clock to get this book completed. Every time I tried to focus or came close to finishing it, life would come along and throw me off my game. "Life would be life'n," as the saying goes. I realize now that timing is everything as I gained more experiences to write about and share with you. God is always on time!

I pray this book blesses at least one person. Maybe it'll encourage someone to keep going while knowing life will not stop happening and time will not slow down. Father Time is undefeated. We must learn to take advantage of slowing ourselves down so that we can take life in while we are living. How we will pour into ourselves daily to keep our heads above water is key. Learning to live and love smarter each day is crucial to our future. Work smarter, not harder. Choosing how you absorb all that life is, has, and will be is what makes all the difference. I disclose intimate details of my life experiences that have shaped me into the woman I am today. I'm still a work in progress, but I do hope that when everyday people like me share their experiences, lessons learned, authentic emotions, love, laughter, tears, pain and prayers, it will help the next person along their journey.

This book is not just about my experiences but for you to incorporate your own, to be reminded to draw off of your own energy and recognize where your level of self-love is. I hope when you finish reading, you are inspired to pour into YOU just a bit more than you did the day before. I hope you lean more into loving smarter as you grow forward choosing to live your best life.

Day #1

TO BE LOVED

*L*ET ME START by saying it is a beautiful thing to be loved. Everyone should have the opportunity to give and receive love. Love is such a powerful word. Showing love is an unmatched expression. To experience the gift of love is life changing. We love in so many different ways and on so many different levels that it's hard to narrow this topic down. Love can truly move mountains. It can also come with pain. Love can build up and restore. Love is amazing, especially once you've learned to love yourself and understand God's love for you. Knowing what love really is to you is important, what it feels like to you. Consider who you love, how you love, and how you should be loved. What do you love? How important is love to you? This chapter is about me learning how to love me and what that really means for me.

I grew up knowing that I was loved by my mother, father,

family, and God, but what I didn't know is anything about truly loving myself. Sometimes I feel as if I am just learning what it means to really love me. When my dad passed away, I was about 9 years old. That is when my male protection was gone. Trust me when I tell you it felt as if every snake in the world got that memo. I had to figure life out without him. I used to do everything with my dad, from hanging at the bowling alley or while he played horseshoes with my uncles and his friends to even watching a little coin gambling in the archway of the block where he hung out just shooting the shit with his buddies. I was a daddy's girl and didn't want to be pried away from him. I had the coolest dad ever in my eyes. I remember how he'd let me "steer" the wheel as if I had control and was driving the car. I always knew since elementary school that he didn't want me around boys outside of my brothers because he loved me so much. He wanted to protect me and my heart from them probably for forever if he had lived that long.

My daddy did not play about me, as I found out in the second grade. A little boy in class had a crush on me. I'm really telling my age when I say we had the yellow phone mounted to the wall where you had to dial one number at a time and wait for it to circle around before you could dial the next number. The cord stretched all around the kitchen to the stairway. The kid told me to say "I like you" to him 100 times. Back then if you got in trouble in school you had to write, "I will not talk in class" on the board or a piece of notebook paper 100 times. I remember sneaking and sitting on the hallway steps like a dummy about to count it out. I got to about the third "I like you" counting on my fingers and all I heard was a click and dial tone. I looked up over the stair banister where I was hiding out while talking and there was my dad holding down the hang-up button. He was on fire. He said, *"Don't you ever tell any boy you like him. He better be knocking on the door to meet me and walk you to school."* I instantly thought my daddy was going to choke this little guy if he was even caught outside playing tag and looked my way. I just knew from that day on the only guy I would say I like or love you to would be my dad.

Growing up in my late teenage years without my male hero was challenging. I feel as if I was searching for someone who was like a father-figure to protect me but when you are mentally confused about boys to men and what that means for you, you have no idea what you are really in search of or what love really is. You're grasping for what you once knew and think you need. My mom tried to shield me as much as she could but when my teenage years began, the lessons of so-called dating and love soon began for me.

As I grew older and after a few failed relationships, I decided to take some time to learn more about myself, God's love for me, self-love, and my heart's desires. I must say that in my chapters of discovering what self-love meant for me, I learned more about ways I needed to "love smart" after the fact, which is why I'm sharing pieces of my love journey. I learned that we must be taught at a young age about loving ourselves from within and what that means. Setting boundaries for ourselves, knowing what we want and deserve, and not settling for less must be top priorities. Yes, relationships come with compromise sometimes, but we need to know how much we are willing to give and take. I had to learn myself, like me, and love me in ways I had never known before. Learning to love me meant learning what things I like about myself. I learned that I love fashion, cooking, art, decorating, crafting, music, DIY projects, painting, traveling, etc. I learned my love language is "Do them all!" I really like being tall, but I used to hate it. I had to spend time getting to like being alone with me before inviting someone else into my space.

To be loved is a beautiful thing, but make sure you love you first. Get to know yourself first. Trust me, it will save you a lot of confusion and heartbreak along the way. The best thing I could have ever done for myself was to learn to love everything about me–flaws and all. Another thing is knowing we are all flawed, and we must give each other grace. There is no perfect person, but there is a perfect person for you out there, including their flaws that you choose to accept. I learned that having hard and sometimes uncomfortable conversations are needed as part of adulting. Any type of relationship must be watered for it to grow. I do believe that had my dad been present during those confusing times, I would've learned a lot earlier than later.

Learning yourself, taking note of your past experiences, and placing God first in life with no exceptions is what will help you to connect to someone equally yoked. I stopped looking at my clock and allowed God to take control of the timing of my life. The one thing we know if nothing else is to pray in detail. Knowing what you want in a partner is very important, and let's not forget what you don't want. I prayed that I would get a partner who agrees with God being at the center of our relationship, someone compatible with my interests who prays for and over me. I prayed for love that feels healthy and mutual. I wanted someone who would have their own interests and hobbies, was financially stable, and who knows himself within.

I wanted him to be confident, supportive, my friend, lover, protector, smart, funny, and God-fearing. I prayed for a man that I am enough for and who sees my worth without question. I learned to keep it real with God.

A wise friend told me to pray for what feels authentically easy and natural as opposed to confusing. So I said, *"Lord, please send me my best friend so we can be silly and laugh at each other."* You know, like laughing about everything that would've normally been a turn-off for most, such as a fart slipping out or when you can feel comfortable and beautiful with no makeup on and in your sweats. When there's nothing perfect about the relationship but it feels perfect because of the imperfections that exist, you're both willing to work on it in order to grow. I think that is good love. What I've taken away from everything I've experienced in relationships across the board is that placing God at the center is where growth will continue. That goes for any and all relationships, from family and friends to your love life. Placing God first is the best decision you can make because then you know everything else will fall into place and in His perfect time. Oh, what a feeling to be loved!

What or who makes you feel loved? What do you love most about yourself?

_____

_____

_____

_____

_____

_____

_____

_____

_____

_____

_____

_____

_____

Day #1

TO BE LOVED

AFFIRMATIONS

☞ I am beautiful not just in appearance, but my spirit is beautiful. I genuinely love to pour goodness into the world. My existence is necessary and people who are like me make a positive difference in this world.

☞ I show up authentically no matter when or where and remain true to myself. The love I give is authentic. I love who I am. I'm not perfect, but I strive to be a better me daily.

☞ God has shown me time and time again how much I am loved. I am so grateful to know what true love feels like. I am confident, kind, and caring. I attract good and kind-hearted people.

☞ I love spending time alone with myself. I like myself as a person. I am worthy to be loved unconditionally. I will never compromise my self-worth.

- I radiate peace, joy, and love in my daily walk. This is my season of love, peace, happiness, and wealth. Nothing can stop where God is about to take me.

- I attract all things beautiful and kind. I am a magnet for goodness. Love will always find me.

- God's love for me is undeniable with my flaws and all. I am intentional about who I spend my time and love with.

- Being kind to others makes me feel beautiful. I attract love because I am love.

- My daily walk is a divine expression of love. I will always choose love, peace, and happiness for myself.

Day #2

STRENGTH

$\mathcal{S}$OMEONE ONCE SAID you never know how strong you are until strength is all you have left. I know this to be true. I can't count how many times I had to learn just how strong I am, and I don't mean that necessarily in the physical way. Countless times I understood the saying that God will never put more on you than you can bear, so I must dig deep and find the strength to navigate through this thing called life.

One of the bravest yet scariest decisions I ever made was relocating from New Jersey to Atlanta in 2009. I was in such a dark place in my life at the time and needed a fresh start. The move meant being further away from my family in Maryland, which was unfamiliar territory for me. I had only been to Atlanta to attend events years prior with celebrity and/or associate friends at that time. Did I mention I had some fancy experiences in my lifetime? For example, one visit to Atlanta came with police escorts traveling around the city. I dipped into high-profile events and bounced back out so when it came time to relocate, I didn't know many people or my way around. I had one cousin who lived in Atlanta at the time and an associate who convinced me to give it a try. I figured, *"Why not?"* I didn't want to end up being the "shoulda, coulda, woulda" person, so I leaped and went for it. After all, at the time it was just my dog, Champ, and me, myself, and I that this major decision would affect. I had nothing to lose, and my mother encouraged me to step out in faith. She has always been the first to want to see me fly far from the nest to explore all the magical possibilities the world has to offer.

Back then, I am ashamed to say, I cared more about what people would say and felt that moving back to Maryland would make me look like a failure. I'd sink into an even darker place. I also realized that I was highly apprehensive about moving back to Maryland because I didn't want to face things I hadn't fully healed from yet. Some of those experiences I had never felt comfortable sharing with my many. You know those things you hold onto and feel they may be best to take to your grave to keep peace amongst those you love? So now here I was, starting a whole new chapter in life with no idea what it would entail. I remember feeling so lost and lonely. I was willing to start from the bottom to work my way up, but I was clueless as to where to begin in the big, new, peachy state. Life events sure can make you feel defeated at times. I stayed with my cousin to get my feet back on solid ground. My king-size mattress had to sit on the floor in one of his bedrooms because my bedroom set was too large for the room I was staying in. It was stored in his garage.

Less than six months in, my cousin decided to move to a whole other part of Georgia and yet again, I had no clue as to where I was in life physically and mentally. I had spent my last dime relocating and had to literally rebuild my foundation. I felt so sad, broken, confused, and numb but my pride didn't want anyone to know. I had to literally drag myself up each day and rely on a little light inside of me that would not go out even when I wanted it to. That was a chunk of strength given by only God Himself, let me tell you. It was a light the size of a pinpoint tucked away so deep within the darkest place of my heart. Every day I had to find ways to make that hole bigger so the light could shine brighter within. It was all I had left. Have you ever felt this way? A renewed strength that I didn't think I had in me started to kick in after I had released myself from my own self-pity. I started to try to find my way back into the world. What were my likes and dislikes? What hadn't I tried or wanted to try? Back when I lived in New Jersey, I was interested in learning about real estate. I took the course and exam, but quickly learned that wasn't for me. I failed that test the first time with flying colors and didn't need to go back. I hear that the majority fail on their first try, but what I realized is that my interest swayed more toward the structure and creativity of the decor for the interior and exterior of homes as opposed to the sale of homes.

While trying to find my way in Atlanta, I considered using my cosmetology and esthetician license to generate revenue. I wanted to do hair wiggery and work with cancer survivors in honor of my late grandmother. I had it all planned out when in New Jersey but didn't have the right support system in place. I had a vision that others didn't see, but just because other people don't believe in you or your vision doesn't mean you should give up on it. So when I moved to Georgia, I took my vision and dream with me. It wasn't easy at all. It took some months to get out of that feeling of depression being in unfamiliar territory. The reality was hitting me that I could no longer hop in my car and take a drive to be in Maryland just a few hours away to visit my family, sit on my mother's couch and eat cherry cheese pie she makes just for me, eat crabs, and have game night with family and friends. Welp, here I was in Georgia, so it was time to start crawling to find my way to my new destiny. I had no idea what that looked like.

I worked part-time at Victoria Secret. It was cool because they had a makeup counter at that time. Through a personal referral, I was connected to a full-time job opening at a Sports and Entertainment company. I'd observed how they would help athlete's start-up companies and write business proposals so that they could learn how to invest and save their money. I'd ask questions and they were never hesitant on sharing the knowledge. Look at God. There I was working at a company with people who wanted to help me start the process of obtaining my own business. I was able to use in Georgia the same business name I started to brand in New Jersey. I thank those who were able to help or support me that didn't. It was through them that I learned to appreciate those who did. God knew best what my unforeseen journey would look like and who should be in it. I also get that nobody must help you with every dream or goal you have. It is indeed their choice. That is what helped me to not have expectations when it comes to people to avoid disappointment and to know that first and foremost, you got to have you like nobody else has you no matter what.

I eventually started to get back on my feet and moved into a townhome in midtown. I remember being told when doing the walkthrough of a particular townhome I was considering that I may want to pick another available unit because the one I was viewing had a window view of homeless people sometimes lingering around nearby outside of the gated community. My friend and trainer at the time confirmed what the property manager stated. She took me there to view the surrounding area at night, so I got to see what they both meant. While viewing the home, I looked out the window and silently thanked God because that could have once been me. What the property agent viewed as an eyesore, I viewed as motivation and an opportunity to help others. I turned to him and said, *"This is the one I want."* The young man looked at me with a confused face. *"Most times, we don't look like what we've been through,"* is what I said to him. Praise God for that! I felt that I had been one step away from that experience and it would keep me humbled. Every day, I would look out the window with a grateful heart. It was a reminder of how quickly life can change and how blessed I was. I thought everything that had happened to me was to make me weak and sink, but it was really making me stronger and teaching me how to swim. A part of my life's purpose would now always be about "Paying It Forward" as someone did for me. I didn't have much, but I would make sandwiches and buy cases of water to take out to the people who would go to the shelter nearby. When my nieces came to visit, I had them join me. I wanted them to understand how fortunate they were and to learn to never judge a person based on their current situation. Listen to their stories and learn from their life experiences. We are all one beat away from not being in the best situations in life, so I try not to judge anyone because I surely don't want anyone judging me.

Eventually this led to teaming up with one of my dearest friends. She started a movement of feeding the homeless in the same location. We'd set up folding tables full of food and water and invite others out to join in serving. We would buy as much food as we could afford to give until we ran out. We'd listen to the homeless and less fortunate people's stories that led to how they got to this place in their life. We must all understand that we all have a story and may be one story away from being in those same shoes. Doing for those who have less than you and not wanting anything in return will bless your soul in an unexplainable way. It will sometimes make you recognize that what you complained about the day before was minor compared to what others are experiencing. The goal for us was to help them know there were people who cared and to give them a sense of renewed strength to keep going and never quit no matter what life throws their way. In return, it also did the same for us.

We could all use a push or an encouraging word from time to time, even from a stranger, to remind us of our own strength even when we are in our weakest of life's moments. We all go through ups and downs and should not be ashamed of that. My amazing friend is now known globally as a mental health advocate, spearheading a major movement in silencing the shame when it comes to asking for help or seeking counseling as one pushes through the challenges we go through in life. Again, I say praise God most of us don't look like what we've been through. To God be the glory for His mercifulness and new grace daily. His second and third chances over our lives are game changers. Having the will and faith to dust yourself off and go through life knowing you are not alone is key. Thank you, God, for giving me the strength to endure hardships, grief, trials, and tribulations so that they would end up being my testimonies used to strengthen not only me but someone else.

To whom much is given much is expected. Was there a time in your life when you felt all you had left was strength from within to push yourself forward? What do you do to give back or help lift someone up to get ahead and find their strength within again?

_____

_____

_____

_____

_____

_____

_____

_____

_____

_____

_____

_____

Day #2

STRENGTH

AFFIRMATIONS

- If it hadn't been for my struggles, I would not know my strength. My inner-strength is just as strong as my outer-strength. I will remain humble and accept my anointing from God.

- God's light will always shine on and in me. His light is my compass. I believe that every shift ahead will lead me to great opportunities.

- I can move mountains with the strength that resides within me. I will live a life thriving and not just surviving.

- I am a student of God, therefore, I have to take the tests I'm given. They are used to prepare me for the next level. My final reward will be so worth it all!

- God's favor and love finds me and those around me. I dwell in the light of the Lord and share my light with others unselfishly.

- Everyday my strength is renewed. I choose to have a good day on purpose despite what my circumstances may be.

- I will live my life with compassion. I may bend like a palm tree, but I will not break.

- With God's love, I am strong even when I feel weak.

- I am meant to live a blessed and fruitful life, and to help others do the same.

Day #3

RECOGNIZING YOUR RESILIENCE

THERE WILL BE TIMES when life will knock you down. It's unavoidable if you are LIVING. Read that again! The key is to get back up and maintain resilience. Although it is not always easy, having the mindset of knowing you have the ability to bounce back can pull you up when knocked off your feet. I have heard "No" more often than "Yes" in my lifetime. I thank God that even though many of the times the answer was "No" and I was discouraged, I never gave up. There were so many times I wanted to give up, but there's some kind of fabric that God stitched me with that won't allow me to quit even when I kick and scream wanting to. A lot of times we don't know how resilient we are or even have the ability to be, but God does. So many times I threw in the towel, and it was thrown right back at me to wipe my tears and sweat. It's that spiritual sign that says, *"Don't give up. You are stronger than you know. I am God, trust me."*

I worked for the State of Maryland for many years straight out of high school. I never personally felt college was for me, although I thoroughly believe in constantly learning and advancing in education in whatever field you have an interest in. I didn't want to put the financial burden of college on my mother as a single parent, nor did I want to incur that kind of debt not knowing what I really wanted to do in life just yet. The state job was within walking distance from my mother's home, which was perfect for me before getting my first car. I didn't tell her this at that time but as I was maturing, I preferred to work and be close to her to help with my brothers and the house over being away at college.

I have no regrets about that decision. I knew I was creatively gifted and had already started working for the Department of Motor Vehicle Administration during my senior year through a work-study program. After graduating high school, I stayed working with them full time. I got to enjoy a bit of college life from visiting my friends and cousins on their campuses. Eventually I started working at the District Courthouse in Glen Burnie, Maryland, then moved on to the Department of Human Resources in Baltimore City working as a disability specialist. My part-time job was senior cashier at Foot Locker, modeling gigs, and doing anything crafty and creative that would make me extra money. This included sewing beads and pearls on my friends' outfits and gluing rhinestones to hats and sunglasses. If you knew me then, you know! I even tried to tap into entrepreneurship like my grandmother, creating

"Sandye's Fashion Trends." I'd make creative T-shirts and sell new and gently used, high- and low-end fashion. I was and have always been a go-getter! People often wonder why I spell my nickname, Sandye, with an "e" after the "y." One of my beautiful and intelligent aunts, who is also my godmother, used to teach Spanish, French, and Japanese. Every year on the front of my birthday cards, she'd spell my name Sandye as opposed to Sandy. I liked that it was different and set me apart from the usual spelling, so I started using it. The "y" has the sound of an "i." It has been my personal staple ever since.

When I was younger, people in my community would sometimes tease me for being tall, lanky, and thin. I had long, skinny legs and wore big Jordache sneakers that made my feet look like boots. I remember being maybe in my mid-teens, standing outside on the curb around a crowd of friends and associates. One boy just randomly pointed to me laughing and saying I looked like a parking meter standing on the curb. Everyone burst out laughing. I admit it was a clever joke but deep down inside, it messed with my confidence. Back then I was silently uneasy about my height and weight. Where I grew up, meat on your bones was the in thing. One of my aunts and my oldest half-sister used to model, which had a huge influence on me growing up. I was a tomboy, but I would play in their clothes. My oldest sister would take me to Epstein's & Value City to buy me popular, name-brand clothes for affordable prices. To this day, that is how I shop. I love to mix high- and low-end priced fashion. For me it's more about personal style than a brand name.

It seemed that my awkward body type fit into the modeling world as opposed to my everyday world at that time so throughout high school and after, I would catch the bus to New York to go on modeling auditions to give it a try. Back then, casting calls were very different. We did walk-ins carrying our portfolio of head and body shots. Now you can just upload photos online across the world. I would spend the day walking New York blocks from agency to agency. I would hear, *"You need to lose weight in your face so drink less water"* or *"You're not tall enough"* or *"This year we are going for the Cindy Crawford look."* I'd use my eyeliner to put a little black mole on my face. I would stop being a tomboy for a day to play in my Aunt Shelly's shoes to feel taller and practice my runway walk, almost breaking my ankles. My grandmother would have me walk with books on my head for fun while practicing. I'd travel all the way to New York just to take the "No" with a grain of salt and get back on the bus to Baltimore and show up to my 9-5 state job in the a.m. The rejection was discouraging as hell, but I would suck it up and spring back. I went through all the "No" responses until I ended up getting a "Yes!" The stubborn Taurus in me was determined to get a "Yes," and was not going to stop until I got it. I needed a "Yes" to help me figure out where I fit in.

I ended up modeling for major brands. I landed my face on the box of Dark and Lovely, and the front page of *Jamaica Fashion,* a weekly local newspaper. Tell me "No" and God will show you why you should have told me "Yes." There is a humble sense of arrogance I believe you must have if you're going to bet on yourself. I must maintain a resilient mindset daily to stay sane. Please don't ever quit on yourself. Self-discipline and consistency are key. Discipline has been one of my biggest challenges. Be persistent in pursuing what you want. Know who you are and be confident in knowing God has your back. Show up for yourself everyday knowing that alone will get you through some of your toughest days. If you don't know who you are, the world will tell you who they think you are and what they think you can and can't do. God made us like palm trees. We bend and may even crack, but we don't break! If for some reason you do break and crumble, trust that God will piece you back together better than before. Sometimes it's not about how quickly we recover from the "No," the rejection, difficult conditions, sickness, loss of a loved one, heartbreak, losing a job, etc. It's about knowing we can recover, bounce back, and spring forward. If you are the only one left who believes in you, then that is enough.

I used to doubt myself, causing procrastination. Procrastination delays your progress. Being resilient does not mean you won't feel the stresses of life, but you do get to choose how you bounce back or deal with them. Stay consistent and keep your foot on necks without letting up, as they say. Even if you don't have the resources, have faith. When you don't have the support, have the energy to push through alone. Look in the mirror and pat yourself on the shoulder for the progress you are making. Nobody knows what it takes to be you. Don't be discouraged if things aren't going as planned. Continue to trust in your vision for your life, your talents, skills, and potential. Keep kicking doors open and walking in, letting people know who you are. Walk in every room with the look of confidence as if God sent you. Even if there is fear in your chest, do it scared and never let them see you sweat.

To this day, I try my hardest not to let anything stop me, not even a "No" and not even me. A lot of times we can get in our own way. If you try to hold me down, the Taurus horns will come out. I will ram my way into any room and demand the "Yes" I deserve.

What difficulty or tough life experience taught you how resilient you are?

_____

_____

_____

_____

_____

_____

_____

_____

_____

_____

_____

_____

_____

_____

Day #3
RESILIENCE
AFFIRMATIONS

- ☞ I can withstand adversity and bounce back. I am becoming the greatest version of myself.

- ☞ I have the power over procrastination. I'm headed in the right direction with my progress. I trust the process of pushing through to reach my goals. I will never fold and give up on me.

- ☞ I will bend every "No" into a "Yes!!" I stand on God's promises for my life.

- ☞ I am resilient and full of optimism. I trust my ability to overcome obstacles. I will turn setbacks into stepping stones. I am not meant to be average.

- ☞ I am a focused finisher and will win against all odds. I can do hard things and will never quit or give up on myself.

- ☞ My legacy will be built from my unwavering resilience. I will not be afraid of what the future holds. I am ready to embrace all the blessings with my name on them!

- God is with me even in my darkest hour therefore, I can overcome all obstacles that come my way.

- I am an executor and committed to getting things done. Nothing can stop me from getting to what God has for me.

- My resilience is what keeps me leveling up daily. I will reach my full potential even if some days are harder than others. I got this!

- I am battle-tested and proven to be a warrior! I am a wise, bad-ass beauty with a kind heart. I will overcome all challenges.

- My resilience is my greatest strength. I am unstoppable.

Day #4

BELIEVE BIGGER

STOP SLEEPING ON YOURSELF and live your life to its fullest! Be a dreamer! Why not dream BIG??? It's free and doesn't cost you anything extra. I always say, "Dream using beautiful, bright and bold colors!" Daydream it and bring it to life. Speak it out loud. There is power in the tongue. Speak life into the things you want. That's why I love reciting affirmations out loud. Words are so powerful. The way you use them will either sabotage your growth or give you renewed life daily, so choose your words carefully. Surround yourself with doers and dreamers. If I'm the smartest person in the room, I better be teaching because if not, I don't belong there. I want to continuously learn.

I have always dreamt bigger than my circumstances. Keep people around you who believe in you and push you into your greatness on days you don't feel up to it or lack self-awareness in just how dope you are. On the other hand, trust me when I tell you there will be times when you can't reach or connect with those people for whatever reasons. That is when your personal relationship with God must kick in. Your love for self must go into overdrive. Knowing that you have God on your side should fuel you up. Looking into the mirror reciting affirmations surrounded by my true inner-belief helped me a lot. I know that God has equipped me with everything I need to fulfill the dreams He put inside of me.

I remember when I was moving into my first beauty business location. It was a small room about 10 × 10. One of my closest girlfriends was hyping me up as if I had just bought a three-story building. She kept saying, "OMG you are going to be so busy San with clients on top of clients. It's going to be great." She balled her fist up with pure excitement and showed a huge smile cheering me on as if she could see the future. I was looking at her with a side eye because her energy was on a trillion, but I was nervous as hell. Not that I didn't believe it could happen over time, but never was I thinking it would really happen in a matter of months. This was the first time I'd ever opened the door to my own business for people to walk through. They say if your goals don't scare you, they aren't big enough. Well once I signed that lease, saw my business name on the outside of the building and took on the responsibility of running my own business, I was scared and excited at the same time. Another good girlfriend showed up with a step ladder to help me put my custom brand decals on the wall and prayed over my space. Another girlfriend and her husband helped put together glass stands to put my licenses and product in. I had to learn and create my own website in the beginning because at the time, I couldn't afford to pay someone.

Everything was trial and error, but who could've known I'd look up in the next few months swamped with clients to the point that I could barely squeeze in time to eat lunch. I was able to start paying for help with making my website, business cards, and pamphlets to look consistently professional. I told my girlfriend she cursed me because I was so busy I couldn't think straight. My head felt like it was spinning off. At that time, I had no system in place for booking appointments outside of receiving and returning calls from clients using my personal cell phone for my business. I was also doing hair for a TV show that required me to travel back and forth to Los Angeles. A dear friend of mine believed in my talent enough for her and members of her family to give me that amazing opportunity. It was such a blessing to stretch out of my comfort zone and be able to hone the craft of being a hairstylist. We were all originally from Maryland, so it was like being with family working. My business started to grow, and I literally found myself overwhelmed, overbooked, and overworked but grateful while trying to do it all. I knew I had to make some changes because I had no work-life balance. I couldn't enjoy dinner out with friends because I was always on my phone responding to clients wanting to schedule an appointment, but I couldn't let it conflict with my traveling schedule or call time while working on the show during their season of filming.

I had to step back and see what was happening. I had to catch up with the level of success I had prayed for. I was being placed in a position to grow my business, which meant having a scheduling system, setting structured business hours, and having a business phone. I believed in the bigger dream but hadn't prepared for it. Entrepreneur life was a beast, but I'm grateful for having to take the around-about in learning how to run a business. Now my blueprint can be someone else's shortcut. One of my clients who became a dear friend brought me some beautiful crystals to keep in my business suite with a note that read, "I attract and gratefully receive prosperity, abundance, and success in my life, and so it is!" I still have that note and the crystals more than a decade later.

One of my dearest friends of more than 25 years was a very popular on-air radio personality at that time and would shout my business out on the strength of love. That helped to place my name and brand in rooms I wasn't even in. When I say surround yourself with friends who genuinely want to see you shine and believe in you, I mean that. When one wins, we all win! Friends and family who want to pay for the service you provide or product you are selling to help your business grow without asking for discounts is a wonderful thing. It's so awesome to have authentic people in your corner sincerely rooting for you, supporting and encouraging you throughout your journey. I love my tribe and the support we give each other. There were times when I had a goal, vision, or idea and it seemed as if God said "No." What I came to learn is that God will say "No" because we are aiming too low, and God's vision for us will require us to reach higher. You truly can live a life of abundance if you work hard, trust God, and believe in the promise of what is for you is for YOU!

The first time I heard of a vision board, I was so excited to create one. Funny thing was, I found myself starting out with adding what I had already accomplished to the board. It was the first time I had really stepped back and looked at goals I had already achieved and patted myself on the back. Places I had traveled to and goals I had fulfilled kind of blew my mind. I included a picture of me after taking the plunge and chopping all my hair off at one point because it was damaged. It was a tough decision at first. I wanted to hold on to the deadweight. It reminded me of my personal bravery in learning to let go of deadweight to make way for new growth. They say a woman is about to change the world when she cuts her hair. I would daydream about having a pixie cut and not feeling so attached to lengthy hair, thinking it contributed to defining who I was. It was a bold and powerful sense of freedom I wanted to feel, and I had done it. I think that some should also explore doing vision boards of what they have already accomplished. Sometimes we forget how far we've come when we're so focused on where we're going.

As I started to do more boards, I realized they weren't large enough for my dreams. Having a creative mind can have one dreaming way past the moon and stars while others are staring at you as if you're crazy. I'm sure Noah building an ark looked crazy to others watching until it started to rain. My assignment is not for others to always understand, and I cannot care about convincing others of what God is telling me to do. I realize my faith can make me look foolish to others, but I'd rather be a dreamer than not. I'm always setting new goals and wanting to try new things. Constantly evolving is key for me. What about you? You'll know if God placed a dream in you because He will supply your every need toward achieving that dream. When you don't know how, a way will be made. If you try to run from it, it will chase you down.

I stopped being realistic when it came to what I saw versus what I imagined. I started believing that anything was possible because my breaking points always turned out to be my break-through moments. I am a unique and fascinating human being. When I look in the mirror, I see my scars and broken pieces. I see what others can't see when they look at me. It looks like a masterpiece of art to me because I know firsthand all the different ways the devil has tried to break me but didn't. Many of us have survived the unimaginable yet still get up every day and press on. Simply put, I'm just a girl from Baltimore who believes! I know that God has placed something special inside of me. I always feel that if I don't believe in myself, then why would anyone else? I have the audacity to believe that I can do whatever I set my mind on achieving. My mother instilled that trait in me at an early age. Why would those who look up to me believe that miraculous things can emerge from dreaming big if I don't?

I used to play into using the words "small business" or "my little" this or that. I don't refer to myself or goals as small or little anymore. I understand that fear can be a natural human instinct when headed toward the unknown. I've learned to do whatever it is even when I think I'm not ready or don't know it all. Sometimes the best thing you can do is to simply start where you are. You may never be or feel fully ready, so just do it! The truth is, I learned that I will never be ready per say. With all the resources out here today, I say learn as you go along. Don't wait to start. The best investment you can make is in yourself because you will be the best project you'll ever work on. Procrastination will rob you blind. If a door is closed, climb through the window. Your skills, gifts, and talents are needed in this world and will make room for you. Place your actions into creating the life you want. I sow seeds as often as I can wherever I can, but I've learned not to expect the harvest to necessarily come from where I've sprinkled my seeds. Don't wait for anything to come in return. Continue to live out each day to the fullest and dream! Even when you don't feel like it, SHOW UP!! If God woke you up, show up!

Why would you not take some time to close your eyes and daydream about the beautiful life you could have? Daydreaming is FREE! The same energy you give to thinking you can't, apply it to Yes You Can! It all starts with your mindset. The road to success is not straight or easy. My journey has been filled with curves, loops, bruises, laughter, tears, unexpected twists, and a gazillion bumps. I'm sure there are more ahead, but I will reach my destiny. If I can dream it, I can do it! I dare you to Dream BIGGER using beautiful bold and vibrant colors. Dull colors can be boring but whatever color you use, make sure you go outside the lines. Even broken crayons color, so what are you waiting for? Do you believe in yourself? Would you bet on yourself if you knew God equipped you with everything you need to fulfill your dreams?

Do you see the beauty in dreaming bigger?
Are you going to do it scared?

_____

_____

_____

_____

_____

_____

_____

_____

_____

_____

_____

_____

_____

Day #4

BELIEVE BIGGER

AFFIRMATIONS

- I do not accept mediocre for my life because I trust the vision I have for the life I want.

- I manifest everything that I deserve and always expect that miracles are headed my way.

- I dream big dreams using bright, bold, and beautiful colors. Dull colors are not allowed in my dreams. My vision is vibrant and full of life.

- I release all fear and anxiety because everything is working for my good. I will succeed at everything I set out to do.

- I'm surrounded by supportive people who shower me with positive energy. Together we deserve to live our best lives. I want to see us all winning.

- I have the power to create the life I want. I speak life over my goals and am headed toward my winning season.

- I am so proud of what I've accomplished and excited by what more I'm going to do.

- I am destined for greatness. I empower and encourage myself through God's love for me.

- I dream big because I believe bigger is meant for me. I'm a creative person, so there are no limits. I have everything to be successful. God's promise to fulfill my dreams still holds true.

- I deserve everything I can dream up because God placed those dreams inside of me.

Day #5

LOVE SMART

IN MY NEW SEASON OF LIFE, I'm determined to live and "love smart" based on what I have learned from past personal experiences. I had never done so because I never learned anything about loving smart. I only knew what it was like to *give* love without considering what I really wanted *from* love. This mindset opened the door to a newfound love I have never explored for myself, my career of choice, or anyone connected to me. Everyone must come secondary to God. After that, I must put myself first. There were times I thought I was putting God and myself first but in hindsight, I can honestly say I wasn't.

Have you ever sat in your authentic truth? Sometimes you must hold yourself accountable for the decisions that you made. I once felt as if I departed from a relationship with nothing but luxury material items and grand travel experiences to list. Yes, that part sounds amazing and it was, but my personal issue with myself was that I held off on things I really wanted out of the relationship to please the other person. They were satisfied with getting all that they wanted at that time in their life. What everyone else wants and when they want it may not align with your needs. I was never a materialistic girl although yes, I like nice things, don't get me wrong. But like most women, as I got older, I learned what's important to me and what isn't. You know what you want and what you don't want to settle for when it comes to your career choice, friendships, and love life. I've walked away from friendships where I constantly poured into the other person but never felt as if I was being poured into. I was only left feeling drained. You may read this a few times, but I am a recovering people-pleaser. It took me years to hold myself accountable for certain situations I had once put myself in or stayed attached to for too long because I wasn't being wise about what would be best for me in the end. I know somebody reading this has been there and done that too. So many times, I thought I was loving and living smart because I was committed and loyal to people or jobs without fully being committed and loyal to me first.

Loving yourself in a smart way is about making sure you can stand on your own if anything should happen. That can be related to your health, job, family, etc. Make smart choices by making sure you focus on your health just as much as you would while caring for someone else's well-being. Keep your house in order before you go clean someone else's. You can love what you do all day long, but are you living smart? Pour into your personal goals the same way you pour into your job or someone else's goals. You can love someone, but are you loving in a smart way to make sure you will be ok in the event things don't go as planned? As an experienced grown woman who has been through some things, I always say have your own. It's not yours if your name isn't on it. All I'm saying is that from my personal experiences, I've learned that loving yourself first in the smartest and smallest ways can't hurt.

Harsh lessons taught me to love smart. Being disappointed because of someone else's decisions was among the best things that have happened to me. Did it hurt? Hell yeah, it did! It was some of the worst pain I've ever felt, but I learned what I would not have understood. It taught me to rely on myself and God above all others. If I let myself down, then I have no one else to blame but me. When friends or loved ones aren't around, God is. One thing I know for sure is that God will never let me down. Become confident in being independent and anything else will be a bonus. I had to learn that putting myself first was a must, not an option. My happiness and self-fulfillment must come from within. I now like being alone with me, myself, and I. Spending time alone is always an eye-opener that allows you to see things clearer. Moments away from chaos to strategize are important before making your next move. It especially helps to block out all the noise so you can clearly hear God's voice to guide you in your choices in life. Do you like you? Do you spend more time beating yourself up about poor decisions you made? Do you say, "I learned from that and know the next time what to do better? I forgive myself and grant myself grace to grow from that experience." Do you tell yourself that wisdom has now been granted to you from those experiences?

When I chose the entrepreneur life, my decision was based on not being in a position to get fired. It was also about creating my own opportunity as opposed to hearing "No" to an opportunity. It was about putting myself in a position of having to rely on me and me alone as I allow God to guide me. I was tired of giving others the power over my life. I wanted to create my career life on my own terms. My thoughts were that if I hired myself, I could never be fired. I wanted to be my own boss and make my own schedule. I wanted to control my own destiny. Entrepreneurship isn't as easy as some make it look but one thing for sure, it is a constant teacher. You are continuously learning to be smarter and do better than the day before.

In all my past personal relationships—whether friendships, love interests or business-related—I vowed to be smarter than I was in past situations. Have you ever found yourself in a business- type relationship? The business mentality for some will keep them pushing on to the next deal on the table if they see things not working out, all while you try to argue the fact that you are a person, not a deal gone bad. I've experienced people turning straight cold with no emotions attached when they weren't getting what they wanted or were jammed up in a corner having to make a solid decision. Some people don't know how to balance business, friendships, and love. For those who do, it probably took them time and moments of trial and error to master it.

I remember a past situation where I desperately started to want more for myself outside of what other people thought should have been enough for me. I had my own personal goals in mind as I watched years flying by. I had all the things but no solid foundation of stability for myself. Sometimes things are enough during a certain season in your life, but you are entitled to change your mind at any time if you desire something different for yourself in terms of personal growth and life goals. I love to help others achieve their goals and truly love to see people reach success, but I was never the person who could be around successful people and not want my own security blanket. Yes, I want a seat at the table, but there is nothing like having your own table and being able to invite who you want to sit at it. I've been around some extraordinarily successful people, which of course made me know that success was obtainable. Instead of expensive handbags, watches, or having fun in casinos, I prefer land and opportunities to build something solid. I like all those things but as I matured and wised up, I wanted something that would help build long-term, concrete security.

In my mid-30s, I decided I wanted to pursue obtaining my cosmetology and esthetician license, so I took out a student loan for my trade school of choice. It was something I wanted to do in high school but couldn't back then so there I was, in my 30s going for it. It was deemed not a good enough career choice for me to choose in others' eyes, but it was what I felt passionately about so I paid half out of my pocket and the other half was covered by a student loan. While traveling and attending lavish events, I studied my butt off, earned my hours, and got my license. It's a billion-dollar industry and you can take those skills anywhere in the world because everyone wants to feel and look good. It's a rewarding career in many ways. Let's be honest, when you look good you feel good. It builds confidence.

I wanted to become a businesswoman with purpose. It was interesting to be celebrated for achieving what I had set out to do by those who thought it wasn't good enough in the beginning. That's why I always say, "Do what you feel is best for you and not what others feel is best for you." Don't let your age or other people's limitations stop you. If you believe enough in yourself, you will achieve your goals with or without others because God will provide if it is a part of your calling. One of the smartest things you can do is believe in yourself. One thing I know is that I must be able to look at myself in the mirror and be good with the decisions I make for me. If you don't make the decisions you feel are best for you, you will hold resentment toward yourself at some point.

Sometimes I have those talks with myself and ask, "Am I thinking smart? Am I in an ongoing stagnant situation or a place of growth for me and my life's desires?" There came a time when I had to acknowledge to myself that people love and support differently, and that is ok. You must learn as you go along in life to choose how you want to be loved and what that looks like for you. What is most important to you and your personal growth is up to you to decide. You can't make anyone do anything they don't want to do or aren't ready to do. I also learned that sometimes when people don't agree with your decisions, you may find yourself facing the ugly side of people. Hurt people hurt people and business is business outside of personal. I learned that verbal agreements hold no weight if it isn't in writing. I'm not sharing this from a negative standpoint. I'm sharing all of this from an awareness standpoint.

Love, family, and friendships mixed with business are good when it is good but when or if you hit a sour spot, it can become a bitter situation. Every individual has a right to feel how they feel and to do what's best for them. I now understand when people use words such as "the business in relationships."

They come with terms and conditions that need to be in writing. For example, I learned the hard way that my name must be on the lease or deed to where I live to feel secure, the business I'm pouring into, and so forth. I share this because my personal advice is to always have your own, love smart, and make smart decisions when it comes to personal and business decisions. People will show you who they are, good, bad, or indifferent. Don't be disappointed if they are being who they are by placing who you are on them.

Life lessons will teach you if you want to be taught. I understand that the path to learning in life is never ending. When learning for more than a decade how to run a business, there came more lessons to learn than I would have ever foreseen. The pandemic taught us all many lessons. For one, it taught me that I needed to think smarter about how I do business just in case the world should shut down again. My primary job was working hands-on with people, and that was taken away for an unpredictable period of time. Like most, I had no back-up plan for how I operated my business. Upon returning back to work, I had to put new rules and regulations in place as it related to running the business for the safety of my health and others. As a Covid survivor and having overcome close-to-death scares in my lifetime, I now make better choices for me and how I choose to live and take care of myself. Now I focus on multiple streams of income as opposed to one, just in case something such as the pandemic should ever happen again. I'm learning to make my creative gifts make room for me. I don't have it all figured out, but my mentality is to move smarter than I did the day before in all areas of my life.

Your choices to put you first won't always please everyone,

but that's the thing: It's not about them as much as it is about doing what is best for you. There's absolutely nothing wrong with being smart about the choices you make that best suit you in any type of relationship from career to personal, no matter how much you love someone or something.

Do you love smart? Do you make the best
decisions for you in your relationships, career,
family, friends?

_____

_____

_____

_____

_____

_____

_____

_____

_____

_____

_____

_____

_____

Day #5

LOVE SMART

AFFIRMATIONS

- ☞ I love thinking for myself. I choose to make the best decisions for me and my life.

- ☞ I trust myself in doing what is best for me. I am smart. I will continuously seek to learn, grow, and glow daily.

- ☞ I will always go where there is trust, love, and reciprocity. I will be wise about who I spend my time with. I deserve genuine love and happiness.

- ☞ I am living my life on my own terms. I choose to love smart. I pray for discernment and ask God for His guidance daily. I am more than enough. I treat others the way I want to be treated.

- ☞ I am an independent person, but I know when to ask for help. I will maintain balance between my personal and business life. I go where I am loved and there is opportunity for growth.

- I am a magnetic force that draws magic near and real love close. Dope experiences arise and unfold right in the palms of my hands.

- I can get the job done alone but know that it is wise for me to accept help if I need it. Asking for help is a sign or strength not weakness.

- I am not perfect, but I am powerful. I choose to stand in my purpose unapologetically.

- I like me and what I stand for. I align myself with like-minded people. I live my life full of peace and love and continuously attract an abundance of prosperity.

- I am my own person, and I highly recommend myself. I am an asset to anyone who allows me to love them.

- I have what it takes to attract healthy and loving relationships.

Day #6

RUN YOUR OWN RACE

AS A KID LEARNING to ride my mini-bicycle, I remember feeling confident because I had training wheels. My dad would push me from behind at a steady pace. It was a step up from the green machine Big Wheel. For Christmas, I got upgraded to a baby blue and white bike that would fit my long, growing legs with a banana boat seat and long, chopper handlebars. My dad would run next to me holding the bike as I pedaled. One day, he let go and I was freely pedaling away not even knowing he was no longer holding me up and guiding me. When I looked to the side and he wasn't next to me but behind cheering me on, I instantly panicked and fell. I begged him not to let go the next time. He told me he won't always be there to hold me up and that I could do it because I had just done it on my own. If you fall, brush yourself off and get back up. He said don't be afraid to do it alone because he'd always be there. He said to stay focused on looking ahead and just keep pedaling, but to also know when to hit the brakes. The things we are taught as kids can carry us a long way in life.

I was such a daddy's girl! I wanted to follow my dad everywhere he went. I grew up in a neighborhood called Cherry Hill in Baltimore, Maryland. We didn't have many electronic games or computers during that time, so we played mostly outdoor games. Red Light-Green Light, Hot Butter Bean, tag, and racing were some of the fun things we'd play. I loved to race my dad around the four corners of the block. "Get on your mark, get set, go!" I would run as fast as I could. I felt like my eyes were half closed. I was running so fast with everything I had in my little, skinny legs. I would slow down to look to see where he was, and I never saw him. By the time I got to the finish line, there was my dad not even breathing hard. He would beat me every time. What I one day figured out was that he would cut across the parking lot and be waiting for me at the start line. Cheating or being clever, whichever you want to call it, when I called him out on it, the point he made has stuck with me to this day. I was out of breath and mind boggled at how he wasn't. He said, "You are slowing down because you are looking to see if you're beating me." He told me to only focus on my race and not his. That is how you win, even if you get to the finish line last. I didn't really get it then, but I do now.

It's interesting because I sometimes must take a social media break. It can play with your head if you allow it to. We must keep in mind that most people don't post their failures, losses, or bad days. More often than not, we see the wins or the "fake it until you make it" posts. Folks don't always share the challenging part of their journey while they are going through it. We start to compare ourselves and think we should be much further along than where we are based on others' races. We get caught up thinking we are supposed to be where they are. It looks all great and like life is easily flowing with success for others, but that is their race not yours. Truth be told, you have no idea what they are going through or have had to go through. Winners focus on winning their race. They understand their own assignment. Distractions cause you to swerve. Stay in your lane. Run Your Race and WIN!

What race are you focused on running in life right now?

_____

_____

_____

_____

_____

_____

_____

_____

_____

_____

_____

_____

_____

Day #6
RUN YOUR RACE
AFFIRMATIONS

- I am my only competition. My only focus is being a better me. I trust God with the pace of my life. I run my own race at my own pace.

- My rate of speed is for me and me only. I have peace by staying in my own lane, minding my business, and drinking water.

- I finish what I start because I pray first, then plan, then pursue based on my personal purpose. Today I will focus on what I want to accomplish. I will execute every assignment like the boss I am.

- I am disciplined and will go the extra mile to achieve greatness. I am constantly evolving into my highest self.

- I will always bet on myself. Even if I fall short, I've already won because I tried.

- I am a winner! Nobody can do what I do the way I do it, and that is my superpower.

↪ Quitting is not an option. I stay true to my core. Today I will put one foot in front of the other going forward and not looking back!

↪ My steps are ordered. Favor, grace, and mercy go before me. Every step I take forward I expect good things to be in my reach.

Day #7

STAY READY

I WOKE ONE MORNING to a loud banging sound. I was about seven years old, if I remember correctly. My curiosity took me downstairs to see what it was. I found my dad in the pantry room off the kitchen building wood shelves. I asked him what he was doing and he replied, stacking canned goods.

Back story: My dad had already survived two heart attacks. He knew how blessed he was to still be around. He also knew that if something happened to him, my mother would be left raising myself and my three brothers to feed, clothe, and care for alone so he made sure his daily routine was solely focused on providing for his family. My father worked for the sanitation company full time and at the local grocery store part time stacking shelves with inventory. As kids, we don't understand the sacrifices our parents make for us to have a roof over our heads, food in our bellies, and clothes on our backs. By the time my dad finished his pantry project, it was full of shelves stacked with canned goods on top of each other from string beans to corn, carrots, peas, soups, and more. On the floor was one of those huge water jugs filled to the rim with coins. My dad was my personal superhero. What I witnessed as a young girl was him leading by example when it came to being a provider and protector.

Every day is not promised. I learned this the hard way in 1981. It was an October day that I'll never forget. I climbed in bed in between my parents the night before. I always felt as if the green-faced wicked witch of the west could never get to me as I laid between them after a nightmare. In the morning, I remember my dad waking and going into the bathroom. I heard him coughing and what sounded like vomiting. Sadly, I knew those signs meant a possible heart attack was happening. I started beating on the bathroom door and tugging on the doorknob calling out, "Daddy, Daddy, let me in to help!" He knew the only way for him to get me away from the door was telling me to go wake my brothers. I ran to my brothers' room yelling out to them and to my mom. Soon after I heard my dad's brown Buick screeching off. My dad knew he was having another heart attack and drove himself to the hospital. Unfortunately, he did not survive the third time.

When I reflect back on my dad, his making sure we had food and coins in the event that something happened to him is one of the examples of what I mean by loving smart. For me, that was a fine example that my dad set. We always say "Stay ready so you don't have to get ready," but do we really exercise this? Although I lost my dad at a young age, I learned many lessons from him that carried on into my adult life. Facing the reality of the inevitable can be very uncomfortable yet it is necessary and important to think beyond your current situation and how something tragic will affect those you love. The one thing we don't like to talk about is the one event none of us will avoid–death. My mother and I have very candid conversations when it comes to such critical topics. As a woman who became a widow and single mother at a young age, she is very expressive about making sure I secure my future. I love how my mom and I are learning and growing together. We live in a fast-paced world where things are always changing. It's interesting as the tables turn with time. I'm not only her daughter and she is not just my mom, but we are also best friends.

After my dad passed, my mother had to learn how to drive that brown Buick. Life suddenly changed into something that wasn't familiar. I felt as if I had to mature fast to be more of a partner to my mom, but I didn't know what that really meant for me at such a young age. I was caught between growing into a hardheaded, smart-mouthed teenager who wanted to hang out past the streetlights coming on and going out thinking I was grown while trying to cross over into being a young lady without a blueprint. When I did reach adulthood, there was so much I wanted to do to show my mom my appreciation for putting up with me. I've been determined to keep my mother up to speed with the growing world of technology. Heck, I'm trying to keep up. We've come a long way from a typewriter and a fat, dial-up computer. I got her an iPad, gave her my old laptop computer, and an iPhone. I told her I wanted her to at least learn the basics of each. I wanted her to have some knowledge of this new world of technology in the event she should ever need it. I wanted her to be able to see the world at her fingertips. So many doubted she would catch onto the new wave of technology, but my momma can show you better than she can tell you. She's so smart, I love it! Now we facetime, talk, or text every day. She is hipping me to new things sometimes now and loves the emojis. We search for new recipes, and she loves using insta-cart.

All I can do is chuckle. She loves seeing how using social media can allow her to interact with her church members outside of church and family she may not get to see often. She can connect with friends she hasn't seen in years and hear how their kids and grandkids are doing. I think she may be getting better at it than I am. But the best part for me having to live in another state away from her is that I get to talk to and see her face every day. I don't play about life and meaningful time with my mom. My one request I have of her is that I talk to her at least once a day. I don't have to talk to anyone else in this world, but I must carve out time to text, call, or facetime her. If she doesn't answer the first time I call, I have a hissy fit making sure she is ok. It tickles her, but I love it!

Are you ready for what's next in your life? Your loved ones' life? Are you ready for what comes next as the world changes? What about that blessing you prayed for? Are you ready to receive it? We should all strive to prepare and be ready in every aspect of our lives from professional opportunities and our health to personal goals. Life can be unpredictable. Are you prepared, equipped, ready, and qualified for what you've asked God for? Start prepping now so you don't have to get ready.

Are you ready, or do you need to start getting ready?

_____

_____

_____

_____

_____

_____

_____

_____

_____

_____

_____

_____

_____

Day #7

STAY READY

AFFIRMATIONS

☞ I stay ready so I don't have to get ready. My palms are open to receive my blessings.

☞ I made a promise to myself to love and live smart. Show me just how good it can get God. I am all in!

☞ God has proven He doesn't play about me, so I stay ready to receive an abundance of success, love, happiness, and peace. I am open to receive all the blessings with my name on them today.

☞ I am committed to showing up for myself. Stress and worries can't control me. Every blessing I receive requires me to pay it forward.

☞ I will leave a legacy for those I love and always do what I want in terms of making me feel self-fulfilled and happy, remembering there are only so many tomorrows.

- I'm ready for major upgrades in my life. I am moving forward with the expectation that something good is about to happen.

- I am well-rested, ready, willing and able to achieve all my goals. I am giving my all when it comes to the life I want. I expect more, so I will continue to show up more than I did yesterday.

- I will pour into myself so that I can pour into others. It is my due season for unexplainable opportunities and miraculous blessings.

- I am a good steward of my time, money, and relationships. I feel God's love all around me daily. God's support surrounds me daily. His love lifts me higher and higher, consistently protecting me. I stay ready for my promised blessings.

Day #8

GRATITUDE

THESE DAYS I WAKE UP with pure gratitude in my heart. I first give thanks to God for allowing me to see another day on this beautiful earth and in my right mind at that. My gratitude for my mother runs so deep. There are so many people I'd want to personally thank for being a blessing in my life, but that's a whole other book. One thing for sure is that we don't get through this journey called life alone. I have truly been blessed in the most unexpected ways at times. God has been so good to me. When I say I have a grateful heart, I am not exaggerating.

Let me tell you more about the time I felt like I was starting life from scratch when I relocated to Atlanta. Well, I was actually starting over in so many ways. Before relocating, I left a lot of stuff behind. I sold a bunch of my luxury bags and watches that carried no meaning going into this new chapter I was entering. Yes, I could use the extra money due to the cost of relocating alone, but it was also a time to release materialistic things that did not define who I was. Detaching from them wasn't hard. How many of us hold on to stuff that we need to let go of, making our load in life heavier than it has to be as we try to move forward? I'm not just talking about material items. I had the mindset that all material items can be bought again, but I understood they weren't necessities.

I used to feel like a hoarder afraid to let go of things and people but as I got older, I learned more and more to release what and who serve me no purpose. There was a time I didn't realize I was carrying a lot of emotional baggage, and it was weighing me down. I was so angry at God for the way my life was going during this transitional stage. I think back to speaking to a kind, God-fearing, and successful associate at that time who knew the way around Atlanta. I sought advice on restoring my faith, renewing my trust in God, and if it was even ok to be angry with God. Have you ever been angry or upset with God? Sometimes you need to talk to a real faithful water-walker who you know has been through some stuff in life to give you authentic guidance on this topic. You can't just go to anybody asking about being angry with God.

I was told to freely be open with my feelings to God, straight no chaser, because God already knows our thoughts anyway. I really didn't know if I would be punished for being mad at God. WHEW!!! And boy, was I BIG mad. I'm flawed, but I felt that I wasn't deserving of things I had endured that caused my life to turn upside down. I'm not a perfect person, but I know I have a good heart and move with good intentions. I felt as if being a good person had gotten me nowhere, and God left me hanging. It was explained to me that we are God's children and my anger was similar to being mad at my parents. We still love them, and they love us. Then they prayed for me and instructed me to stop by the next day to pick up a package from their front gate while they were at church. After picking up the package and driving about a mile away, my cousin was curious to know what was in the envelope. I said it feels like a bunch of brochures probably letting me know where to order takeout from since I was new to the area. I'm laughing and shedding tears as I write this because I had no idea that I was about to be randomly blessed in a major way. It tickles me in how swiftly God can change your circumstances through others, and you won't even see it coming. Let me just say it was a lot of bubble wrap and a generous, unexpected gift. Even though I tried to return it, it was successfully set up so that I couldn't.

They said they had seen me do and be good to others, and that God put it on their heart to do something for me; and that when God tells them to do something, they are obedient. Receiving is very uncomfortable for me because I am usually the giver. That was more than a decade ago in circa 2009. I saw this "Earth Angel" briefly maybe once or twice in swift passing, so to express my gratitude the only thing I could do was and is to pay it forward. Do you know, I still have that same envelope with my name scribbled on it and bubble wrap in a safe place? That should tell you how much it meant to me. I add to it when I can no matter how big or small and use it to randomly bless someone. I always thought that when someone gives they usually want something in return, but there are still people in this world who do good with no ulterior motives or hidden agendas. They sincerely want to see you excel, and that is why they will continue to be blessed. My gratitude runs deep.

Can you think of a time in your life when God sent an unexpected blessing through someone else? I call them "Earth Angels." Have you been a vessel by paying it forward?

_____

_____

_____

_____

_____

_____

_____

_____

_____

_____

_____

_____

_____

_____

Day #8
GRATITUDE
AFFIRMATIONS

- I am grateful for all the kind acts that are coming my way. I attract good-hearted people and good vibes.

- I am deserving of every good thing that is coming my way. I dare not look back because grace and favor are in my present view.

- I am grateful for all my blessings. I will always pay it forward. I must keep going because my best days are in front of me. I operate from a place of gratitude.

- I will wake each morning full of gratitude. I will live, love, and be of service to others. I will always show my appreciation for the kind acts that others show me.

- God is so faithful to me. My God has never left me without. I am so grateful for all that I have. I will step into every new day with an open and grateful attitude.

☞ I am grateful for God's love, strength, protection, and guidance. I operate from a place of gratitude and high frequency. I surround myself with positive people who appreciate life.

☞ I give thanks for my health, peace in my heart, having a sound mind, and knowing that God's love is covering me daily. Today, I will go above and beyond to reach my goals.

☞ Things may not be perfect, but I am thankful that things are coming together for my good and that God's timing is perfect.

☞ Goodness, grace, and mercy follow me.

Day #9

FAITH

HAVE YOU EVER LOST YOUR FAITH? I most definitely have. Since I'm being honest, I have done so several times. I had even secretly in my head written God off, but I'm so glad God never gave up on me. There have been times when I questioned God. Why me? Why did you let this happen to me? Where are you? I would literally holler out to God with anger, wanting to hear His voice to calm me. There were times when I would sit in my car and beat the steering wheel with tears flowing and me screaming at the top of my lungs waiting for God to show up. Humans have let me down more times than I can count, and I needed for my God to pick me up. Each time I thought God left me down, it was only God that could have lifted me up. Sometimes when we are going through storms, we don't see that. That's why I'm here today to share my testimonies.

I had a praying grandmother and on top of that, my mom is a prayer warrior. My mother is the most faithful, God-fearing woman I know. I've seen her go through the trenches of life, but never once did her faith waiver. Truth be told, there were times I didn't understand how a woman could endure so much yet still have faith. It took me a long time to understand personally that faith is all we have to stand on when the blinds are pulled down and we seem to be surrounded by nothing but darkness. There were times when I didn't have the momentum to pray for myself, but thank God for friends and family who prayed for me. I still call my mom to this day and ask her to say the rosary for me. Sometimes it takes an army to go up against the devil. I've also learned that most things we stress ourselves out about, God had already figured it out for us and brought it to pass.

I had to go through some near-death health issues, terrible auto accidents, and money shortage situations. I endured non-trustworthy people, narcissistic folk, fair-weather friends and family and then some in order for me to learn to trust God and His timing and lean on Him. There were times I'd pray for something in particular and God didn't give it to me, although I thought I was deserving. Later I would find out God had bigger and better things for me. Through the years, I have had to learn to match my faith with the enormity of my goals. Every time I feel life is trying to bury me, I remember that I am the seed and the root. I would question if God really loved me at times because I would feel as if God disappeared when I was at my lowest and then BAM, God would show up right on time, literally in a nick of time by the second hand on the clock. It would be done in a way and timing that I could ONLY give the glory and praise to God!

I don't put a specific label on my current spiritual status, although I was baptized Catholic as a child. In my adult years, I started going to a Baptist church in Maryland. Both will always give me a sense of a "church home" when I go back to Balti-more. As I grew older and relocated from one state to another, I visited many churches and streamed online, but I found I had to practice developing my own personal relationship with God. Currently, I choose to maintain a personal one-on-one relationship with God. I focus on being a spiritual being connected with the most high. Some things are unexplainable, and that is when you know there is a higher power working on your behalf. I believe in the universe giving back what you put out. I believe in the connection of energy.

I worship at home in my kitchen, in my car, or whenever the spirit hits me to give praise and thanks. I don't solely rest my walk with God in people. I do believe they are vessels in spreading the word, but no human is without flaws. I have talks with God and listen for God's voice and guidance. If I feel unsettled in my spirit, that means I have unconsciously distanced myself from the most high and need to draw nearer to God. It's so easy to stray, especially when things are going well and there is smooth sailing. I'm not here to judge anyone else's walk, but I'd rather believe in God than not. When I look back over my life, there has never been a time that God has not been there for me.

When some see a field filled with weeds, God sees beautiful dandelions for you to make a wish with. God's love for me has opened my eyes to see that I can make a million wishes in a field of dandelions. I make wishes because I believe they can come true. God hears what we wish and pray for. It may not come when we want it to, but it will come on time! I may jokingly use the word "luck" but that's only because my "lucky charm" is God. I have faith the size of a mustard seed that can move mountains. My faith had become so weak and fragile at one point that I felt I couldn't see the light of day. My faith is now stronger than it has ever been. When I was young, my mother gave me a poem on a wooden plaque that I still have to this day called "Footprints in The Sand." I know God is always there by my side, even when I don't see Him. That's the kind of faith I have.

Do you lean on your faith? Was there a time when you lost your faith? How did you restore it?

_____

_____

_____

_____

_____

_____

_____

_____

_____

_____

_____

_____

_____

Day #9

FAITH

AFFIRMATIONS

☞ My faith is stronger than my fear therefore, I trust the process. Today I will move with faith and not fear. I let go of that scarcity broken mindset. I attract peace, love, amazing opportunities, success, and an abundance of prosperity into my life.

☞ God is faithful to me and has never let me down. I may not be able to see it, but faith says this is my season of mind-blowing opportunities and abundance.

☞ I will trust the process because I know God has my back every step of the way.

☞ God is my trusted source when it comes to all the possibilities I see for myself. God has something so big coming my way.

☞ I don't have time to sit with fear. My own words can empower or destroy me. I will tap into my most courageous thoughts and use my faith to make room for my blessings. I deserve all the good things coming my way. My faith and optimistic mindset will only lead me to greatness.

- My faith helps me to release my frustrations and crushes my doubts. I'm not tussling with negative thoughts. God is working on my behalf, and I am intentional about the beautiful path I am traveling.

- My faith helps me to exceed my expectations and shines through even in my darkest hour.

- Thank you, God, for being my compass. Thank you for always guiding me and holding my hand through the darkness. You always anchor me in safety. I am so proud of my progress, seen and unseen.

- I trust that you are guiding me into a season of miracles. Blessings that I can't see await me. Great is thy faithfulness. Stretch me today, Lord. I'm grateful for all you see in me that I have not seen in myself yet. I'm ready for more personal growth and achievements.

Day #10

FORGIVENESS IS FOR YOU

I T TAKES A STRONG PERSON to forgive, especially for those who never received an apology. I knew I had matured when I realized that every situation didn't need a reaction. I learned the power of silence. I learned how to be calm in the middle of chaos. That is when I clearly saw God showing up and out. The times when I prayed for God to step in, I was able to see God work on my behalf when I stepped back and left whatever situation I was facing alone. So many times, I asked for God's help but couldn't be patient enough to sit still and let God be God. I've also learned that every disappointment has led me toward a different direction that I would not have chosen had I not experienced that disappointment. God's deflection can be for your protection. I have been disappointed and forgiving way too many times to count when it comes to people. I used to take a lot of stuff personal when the reality is, a lot of what people do is not even about you. Some can be about their own insecurities or personal issues. Disappointments can be a setup for something greater if we use the experience correctly and apply the lessons learned accordingly. I used to allow disappointments to distract and discourage me and even take me out of character. Not to say that things still don't shake me up, but I try to stay in control of what I can actually be in control of.

You ever think about the discouraging moments and times people have let you down or hurt you, whether it be at a job, a friendship, relationship, family member, etc.? Heck, have you had to forgive yourself? I have, and it wasn't always easy. I was so down on myself when I couldn't buy that car or house I wanted because of poor financial choices I made. There were times I was beating myself up for not being further along than I felt I should be in my career choice or weight goals. Other times when I stayed in toxic relationships for too long, I held resentment toward myself for a long time afterwards. Things I prayed for I would end up messing up so I started praying to God that if I was blessed with what I prayed for, I would also be given the discipline not to mismanage it. I'm still a work in progress when it comes to forgiving people who have hurt me, but I learned that if you let God handle the karma, you don't have to do anything but carry on with your life. Forgive, for you. Learn from it and move on. Apply those lessons along the way going forward. I know it's easier said than done, but God's timing has always exceeded my expectations when karma slips are being given out. God's timing has always been ON TIME!!

New mercies have been given to me time and time again. I'm so grateful for the power of forgiveness.

We must thank God for closing doors we would have left open. Thank God for redirecting us toward what is better for our health, wealth, and destiny. I forgive myself for the times I accepted less than for myself. I forgive those who lied and hurt me for their selfish reasons. I even forgive myself for any poor decisions I may have made throughout my journey of learning. I now accept that I didn't know what I didn't know. When we know better, we do better. We must treat others how we want to be treated. Forgiveness does not mean that you must embrace or stay connected to what hurt or disappointed you. Set your boundaries and keep pushing. They have probably moved on and are not even thinking about the hurt they brought upon you. That employer has most likely hired someone, and so on, so dump that extra load off of you. That's the best part about forgiving: It frees you from carrying that baggage!

Healing doesn't mean forgetting. Don't be distracted by hurt for so long that it throws you off course and interferes with your peace. Disappointments can lead to a clear discernment. I used to have a "payback" mindset. God will reward you publicly for the pain you endured privately, this I know. You don't have to go and give a reaction to every action. You don't have to prove a point in every instance or clear your name when being lied about. God will remove people out of your life due to conversations He heard, and you will never know why. Just trust that God has your back even when you aren't around. There were so many times I felt as if I needed to speak my truth about certain situations but if you really sit in the power of silence, you won't have to because all will reveal itself in due time and in your favor. At the end of the day, nobody should get to leave a bad mark on you and decide how you should tell your story or heal from it. You can also forgive and speak your truth if and when you choose to. It's your life and your journey. You have control over how you heal and choose to forgive.

Have you heard the saying, "People left when the house was falling apart, not knowing I was tearing it down to build a mansion?" I just wanted to see who left to go grab a hammer to return to help. When people show you who they are, believe them. Not everyone is meant to continue into your next chapter. Not everybody is good for you or wants the best for you. Be ok with that. Not everyone who comes across your path will treat you right or do right by you. Some are there to disappoint, but it is their loss. No need to hold a grudge. Be happy you got to know who to take along with you in your next season and who not to. Carrying all that extra weight is unhealthy.

What baggage are you still carrying that you need to let go of to set yourself free?

_____

_____

_____

_____

_____

_____

_____

_____

_____

_____

_____

_____

_____

_____

Day #10

FORGIVENESS FOR YOU

AFFIRMATIONS

- I practice forgiveness because it frees me. I operate from a place of peace. I will no longer let fear, hate, disappointments, or anxiety hold space in my life.

- I purposely choose happiness and set myself free of carrying anything that weighs me down. This will be one of the best chapters of my life.

- I forgive myself for the times I let myself down, for my past mistakes and self disappointments. For the times I didn't choose me first, I forgive me.

- I release anything that feels heavy on my heart, weighs my spirit down, and tempers with my progress. I am in control of my emotions and thoughts.

- I choose to feel great about myself and my decisions. I set boundaries and stick to them for my own peace. Everybody can't go with me to the new levels God is taking me to, but I will always keep them lifted in prayer.

☞ I am unapologetically my authentic self no matter what. I choose to forgive because favor follows me.

☞ The happiness that I am experiencing since forgiving myself and others feels so good because no one else is controlling it. I will continue to go where I am valued, respected, and loved. Creating healthy boundaries is a major game-changer for me.

☞ From this day on I am solely focused on peace, healing, and growth.

Day #11

HEALING

’M LEARNING THAT healing is a process. From physical to mental, it requires inner self-work to be done. The longer you put it off, the more whatever "it" is will have control over certain areas in your life. You cannot become who you are truly meant to be unless you start your healing process. I do believe that healing can take a lifetime, which is ok as long as you are doing the work each day to take a step further in filling in the cracks of whatever broke you. You must love yourself enough to know you deserve to heal. Sometimes we carry past traumas into our present. It is important to dig deep within and be honest with yourself about the baggage you are towing. It affects our current situations whether that be with work, friendships, our social lives, or relationships. Although I once had a very deceiving experience when I tried counseling for the first time, I still recommend it. In fact, I encourage counseling.

My experience is something I am still trying to heal from, but I am willing to try counseling again even though I am terrified about opening up to someone all over again with this open wound. There is nothing worse than trusting what professionally looks and feels like a safe space only to find out everything was left on the table to share with someone else. The deceit is both devastating and traumatizing. I do, however, know great counselors/therapists who take their job and the oath of confidence extremely seriously. It was already hard for me to trust anyone, so to be brave enough to try counseling and be vulnerable only to find out the professional wasn't being professional was extremely disheartening. I hope that woman is not currently practicing in Atlanta or anywhere else. This world needs too much healing to have that foolery out there. The last thing that is needed is those types of professionals cutting wounds open deeper for those of us who want to heal. Healing from trying to heal is a whole other process, let me tell you.

I believe that we all need therapy even if it's with a trusted best friend who can be patient, listen, not pass judgment, and be loyal and honest with you. Or your way may be by paying someone who is professionally equipped to help you. I just know that keeping stuff bottled up inside can literally cause you to get sick. I don't know if we ever heal completely from certain experiences, but I do know personally that healing requires self-work. I had to get out of my own way to heal when it came to a lot of things. I saw a quote that said quit letting who you were talk you out of who you'll become as you heal.

For many of us we may need to heal in different areas of our lives. The older I get the more I learn that healing brings a certain type of unexplainable peace. I have been figuring out what makes my soul feel like it is healing and happy. I find that laughter always helps me. They say laughter is good for the soul. It keeps you young at heart. I love a good ole from the gut down under belly laugh. I know it's hard to laugh sometimes when you are carrying pain, but it will help you to forget about the pain in that moment. Sometimes we need a moment to let go, release, and be free of the weight we carry. I found that journaling is very helpful. Writing this book has been very therapeutic for me in many ways. I suffered a lot in silence so being vocal and sharing pieces of my life's journey out loud is healing. Most times when we are broken, we forget our worth and somberness hides behind our smile. When you start to feel your wounds healing and you've faced those broken areas in your life, your value is not up for negotiating. You Know You Are Worth IT! Been Worth IT! And no doubt about it... Will Always Be Worth It!

I had to get comfortable knowing it is ok to restart, restrategize, repair, rejuvenate, refocus and rest as many times as I needed to. I sometimes play a gospel song that moves me to tears because I know it's time for a deep cleanse. Sometimes we need to release built-up emotions or anxiety. Do you have one of those songs? A song that you know is going to take you "there?" I used to be afraid to go there. Now I let go and let GOD! I allow myself to feel it ALL. I take it in and absorb the words and feelings that it brings out of me. I let past hurts pass through me. I scream, cry, shout, get on my knees, and praise God for keeping me through it all. It's ok to allow yourself to feel and then release an ugly cry. I emotionally purge often. Running from my emotions has never helped me at all.

It will all catch up and crash down on you making you feel paralyzed when you least expect it. When we try to escape and run from things we need to heal from, we are doing ourselves a disservice.

If it doesn't kill me, then I have a chance at healing from it. As I heal, I am meeting the best versions of myself. I receive God's healing powers over my life. As long as I am alive, I will continue to thrive and push past pain and disappointments and focus on healing open wounds. I always say just because it doesn't take much to make me happy doesn't mean I deserve the bare minimum. And that goes for what I pour into myself. So I'm on a continuous journey of healing. Life be life'n as they say. I have been torn apart at the seams but as I am healing and holding God's hand this go round, I can honestly say you don't know this new me. God put me back together differently. Always remember even broken crayons still color.

What do you need to heal in your life?

_____

_____

_____

_____

_____

_____

_____

_____

_____

_____

_____

_____

_____

Day #11

HEALING

AFFIRMATIONS

☞ I am healing more and more every day. My scars are beautiful testimonies showing that. I have been battled-tested but survived. God has seen the worst in me and still loves me. God's healing powers put the pieces of my mind, soul, and body back together making me feel healed, healthy, and whole.

☞ Even if pieces of me are broken, I am beautifully being put back together. I grab ahold of peace and carry it with me daily.

☞ I accept my past, living my best life today and boldly walking into my future.

☞ I have strength to keep going even when I don't feel like it. I am putting in the work to heal the areas of my life that need fixing.

☞ I forgive myself where needed and will not self-sabotage myself. I let go of all self-shaming. I take accountability of my own actions and embrace my journey of self-discovery and healing.

- Wherever I am planted I will bloom, even if it's through the cracks of cement. I am constantly evolving. My transition while healing is a beautifully seen expression of my personal growth and transformation. I am looking back daily, thankful for never giving up on myself. Everyday I get closer and closer to my true self.

- God's hands will always mold me back into a better me. The pieces of me are uniquely glued together by God's love. I am confident in my ability to make comebacks after being broken.

- God will always lead me with clarity and not confusion. I will step out into today feeling whole and at peace within.

- Healing looks good on me. I will continue to put in the work that is needed. I am free to be a new and better version of myself daily.

Day #12

SELF-CARE

THE FIRST TIME I REALLY learned about self-care, I was playing youth basketball for St. Veronica Church's all girls' basketball team in Baltimore. I played forward and center positions. This was a time when I could appreciate my long legs. I remember we had an away game and were on the bus headed back. I smelled something sour like onions. We were all sweaty after playing our hearts out and winning that game. I kept laughing and saying, "What is that smell!?" Who has a sub with onions on it?" My teammates would crack up because we could all smell the funkiness, not realizing it was us. When I got to my grandmother's house, I realized our under arms were collectively reeking. The smell was not a submarine sandwich with onions, lol.

My grandmother immediately made sure I took a shower. She said to scrub under those arms really good. It was time to learn about deodorant. She sat me down and had a talk with me about how I was maturing into a young lady, which meant I had to learn how to maintain my personal hygiene. Back then, we'd pile on baby powder looking like we had been playing in flour with the rest of our skin glistening from Vaseline because being ashy was a big "NO." It was the start of truly getting a whiff of self-care at an early age. I started watching my mom's routine and asking questions such as what was that big round thing that squeezes water and vinegar out in your top drawer. Nowadays doctors don't recommend flushing out bacteria that our bodies need, but if you know what I'm talking about then you know. As I got older, I learned to love on me by pampering myself with facials, spa days with massages, drinking more water than wine, clean eating as much as possible, waxing, exfoliating, and lathering up my skin with sensual oils and nourishing lotions daily. It is a must for my self-care regime.

As a teenager, I remember when my mother would get home from work. She would sit in the driveway in the car for about 15 minutes before coming in. I was wondering what she was doing because we didn't have cell phones then. She told me it was her moment to pause and be in a place of peace before the chaos, her moment to be still in silence to recalibrate after basically leaving one job before going to another. I can only imagine how taking care of four kids as a single, widowed mother was a job even if it was a home of love. We recently discussed this and fell out laughing because now I do the same thing. I sit in my car just thinking, praying, or simply in a peaceful daze after a long day before going in the house—and I don't even have kids. It was her peace of mind and moment of stillness between work and walking in the door to four rambunctious kids.

As an adult, I understand now the part of being in a safe place of peace and stillness. We all need to take a beat every now and then to refuel. Sometimes just taking a moment to decompress is a form of self-care. A little tender loving self-care is clinically proven to help with anxiety and depression. It reduces stress and the risk of illness. I'm by no means a professional at this, but I also feel that sometimes taking a break can lead to a breakthrough. We perform at our best when we are well-rested and mentally in a good space. Sometimes we need to make ourselves slow down because trust me, if you don't your body will. Been there, felt it, lived it, survived it, never want to feel that way again. Usually it is at the most unexpected and awkward times that God will stop us in our tracks because if it was left up to us, we would keep going and going.

In the past when I would go through the storms of life, I would allow stress and anxiety to keep me up all night. My days and nights were filled with worry. I remember reading somewhere about how butterflies rest during storms because the rain can damage their wings. That always resonated with me. It took a very long time for me to learn how to let go and rest during storms. Worrying was causing more damage than what I may have been worrying about. I had to practice the mindset of understanding that the sun will shine again, a rainbow will appear, and I'll spread my beautiful wings and fly again. Life is always going to throw curveballs. There will be people and situations that will come along to steal your joy and smother your peace if you allow it. Nowadays I work on things that people can't take from me such as my mindset and my well-being. I have a new obsession for my own personal self-care. I put myself first and don't feel bad about it. This takes the highest level of discipline I have ever had to use. I'm no good to anyone if my cup is empty, but there was a time that all I knew how to do was pour into others.

The word "No" is a form of self-care for me. I used to try to attend every event, birthday party, celebratory dinner, outing and brunch gathering, go into work earlier or stay later sick and all to accommodate others with one eye open. I was completely burnt out between work, clients, family situations, relationships, friendships and hell, just life. I would sometimes reach a point of complete exhaustion and still push myself until I had nothing left for me. I had to start saying, "Listen, I wish I could make it but..." If you know my heart, you know me and will not take it personally. I started resenting myself for putting everyone else first. My struggle with myself was real. Everyone else was putting themselves first, no questions asked or explanations given, so I started to question why I felt so uncomfortable doing what was best for me. Being in the beauty industry, people can sometimes unknowingly be selfish. We live in a predominantly vain world. Not saying that is a bad thing because we most certainly should care about how we look which affects how we feel, but can we please have some compassion for those who work tirelessly to beautify you?

The pandemic shook up a lot of folks. Some folks hadn't seen themselves without some beauty enhancements in years. It forced people to look in the mirror and love their authentic selves. For years, I would crawl into work sick because clients would low-key or jokingly make me feel guilty about not feeling well. They wanted me to enhance their beauty today, but please wait to die tomorrow. I chuckle, but that is how it felt at times. I knew most of my clients sincerely loved me but truth be told, if something happened to me, they would find somewhere else to go to get beautified. They'd talk about how nice I was as I laid in the ground. I say that with laughter, but I'm so serious. I know some of y'all beauty professionals feel me. For hairstylists, make-up artists, barbers, bartenders, etc., it's like being a counselor and not getting paid for it. These professions provide a safe outlet for many to vent or share. I would have 10 clients a day with 10 different scenarios from cancer survivors to cheating scandals, happy to get a new job, hating their job, dating stories, losing a loved one, experiencing a client having hot flashes, and happy and sad stories. I would go home drained, and I didn't understand why because I loved what I did. I'm an empathic person so I had to learn to leave work at work, which is challenging. I'm naturally a very compassionate being, so I had no idea how to not show up for others and their situations in a temporary setting and leave it in the workspace. I had my own baggage to carry when I clocked out. Some clients over the years became associates who I truly care about. I must be honest: I prayed for years to God to be able to take a sabbatical so when the Covid pandemic shut everything down, it was an answer to my prayers in a weird way.

As a Covid survivor with long-hauler and prior lung issues, I wouldn't have wished that deathly sickness on anyone. But I was grateful to have time off to allow my body to fully rest and heal. I needed to recharge and reset. Being an entrepreneur, you usually don't have paid sick time. I didn't have to feel the guilt of telling clients I was unavailable or feel bad for not attending an event if I was really exhausted. I got to do things I normally wouldn't have had time to do such as paint and explore other creative talents and hobbies that bring me peace and make me feel happy. Sometimes we need to take a break away to detach from the everyday normal to take time to love ourselves. Normalize not feeling bad for putting yourself first.

Taking a step back can help you find the balance in moving forward. I went through survivor's remorse for a long time. I didn't know what it was that I was experiencing at first. The guilt of surviving a sickness that took so many innocent lives had me confused, depressed, and redefining my life's purpose. I had already survived being exposed to deadly mold, double pneumonia, a horrible car accident where the car flipped three times landing upside down, and then some. I didn't understand why God allowed me to live through that horrible sickness that almost took me out as kids lost parents and parents lost kids. Having to watch the number of deaths happening daily made me go through so many different emotions. I would ask God why I was kept here. I needed confirmation in knowing what my life's purpose is truly supposed to be about.

There is something about a near death experience that changes you. Your appreciation for life and self-care is next level because you know without a doubt it can be gone within a flash of a second. I stopped questioning God and started to focus on figuring out how to live my best life. I started dancing in the rain. I literally go skipping and jumping in puddles like a young girl at heart. I also learned when to rest during storms like butterflies. It's a way of making sure their wings don't get damaged knowing that when the sun comes out again, they will resume flying freely. I find ways to pamper myself by polishing my nails, listening to my favorite music, taking in the aroma from good-smelling candles, and just enjoying the simple things in life. Sometimes I put on music that makes me want to dance like no one's watching as I sing into my hairbrush. Hey, that's cardio at its best. Having fibrocystic breasts, I make sure my mammograms are scheduled. Sometimes I get all dolled up in a fancy-dress, clip-on ponytail and makeup with nowhere to go but to my living room. I take a selfie with my favorite red lipstick, raspberries, and a glass of champagne. I even pop open the good stuff like it's a special occasion and honey, I simply celebrate the blessing of just being alive. You must like yourself to love yourself, and that is where your self-love begins. Don't save anything for a special occasion. As long as you are breathing, that is a special occasion. Start normalizing self-love on a daily basis and thank God for it.

What kind of self-care are you going to start doing?

_____

_____

_____

_____

_____

_____

_____

_____

_____

_____

_____

_____

Day #12

SELF-CARE

AFFIRMATIONS

☞ I will unapologetically fill up my own cup today. I will treat myself with kindness and accept nothing less for myself.

☞ I love myself with everything I have in me. I'm done with putting myself last. Today is all about loving me.

☞ I vow to always love myself through the good and the bad. I promise to be good to myself. I light up rooms when I enter them. I bring the sunshine that others need and I love that about myself, but my first priority has to be me in order to do that for others. Today I will pour extra love into myself.

☞ I love the skin I am in. I go after everything that sets my beautiful soul on fire. I give myself the freedom to have a "pamper myself" day: I do nothing but relax, rest, and reset the day. Today I grant myself the grace to do what I want for me.

☞ It is okay for me to take today to do nothing but relax, rest, and refuel. I give myself permission to slow down and smell the roses.

☞ I allow myself to rest and reset as many times as I need to in order to show up as my best self. Replenishing my mind and body is a necessary requirement on my to-do list.

☞ When I am feeling good and well rested, my energy is a whole other vibe! Somebody is gonna catch this joyful vibe today. My energy is going to be contagious all week.

☞ I owe it to myself to put myself first and shower myself with love and undivided attention. I will celebrate today as if it is the day I was born.

☞ I will cherish and take care of this temple God has given me. I will nourish it with love and plenty of water. I will feed it with only things that will keep it positive, healthy, and thriving.

☞ I will responsibly take great care of myself mentally, spiritually, and physically.

☞ I am strong, brave, beautiful, resilient, creative, powerful, confident, and enough.

Day #13

CROWN ME QUEEN

ONE OF THE MOST memorable experiences of my life was having the distinct honor of being in the presence of queens and living legends who I so admired. Amazing, iconic women who have paved the way for me and so many others all under one roof, and little ole me in the same room with them. I give God all the glory for allowing me to be a plus-one in attendance. It's such a beautiful thing when I see women complimenting each other, lifting one another up, and fixing each other's crown. I experienced this in such a magical way that it still feels like a dream. To this day I still get asked about how amazing it was, which is why I chose to share this significant piece of my journey.

I was blessed many years ago to attend a Ball for Legendary Women! The queen of all queens, Opray Winfrey, chose to have a three-day celebration honoring those who came before her. That weekend became officially known as "A Bridge to Now: A Celebration of Remarkable Women in Remarkable Times." The event honored 25 amazing African American women in art, entertainment, and civil rights. I had no idea how this one weekend would end up changing my life. Can you imagine being in the same room with iconic women such as Maya Angelou, Coretta Scott King, Cicely Tyson, Toni Morrison, Diana Ross, and Tina Turner, just to name a few? There were queens including Janet Jackson, Ashanti, Mary J. Blige, Mariah Carey, Missy Elliott, Susan de Passe, Felicia Rashad, Patti LaBelle, Halle Berry, Iman, Chaka Khan, Natalie Cole, Angela Bassett, and the list goes on. I had to pinch myself.

The younger queens read a poem to the magnificent, seasoned queens who helped pave the way for them. The poem, "We Speak Your Names," was written by Pearl Cleage. There was not a dry eye in that place! Oh, what a magical weekend it was! So many phenomenal women who I highly respect. My God, it was beyond anything a little Black girl from Baltimore could dream up. I get teary-eyed and chills on my arms just reminiscing. The excitement I had when I called my mother to share this experience brought her and I both to tears. I got to dance next to the Obamas on the dance floor so yes, I have bragging rights in saying I met the first Black president of the United States of America before he was. Whoop whoop!!

But in all seriousness, I'm just here to say God is good! The essence of sisterhood that took place soothed my soul. I thank God for allowing me to experience such a precious moment in time that will never be forgotten. Listen here: God will place you in rooms that will blow your mind. I left understanding part of my life's assignment. I was forever changed. I was on a humble high! I felt an extra dose of confidence enter my posture. I knew without a shadow of a doubt I was a woman destined for greatness after that weekend. I am supposed to walk amongst courageous, dignified, queens who carry themselves with poise and class, women of strength with gentle spirits who showcase grace effortlessly. I'm always ready and willing to learn from those who came before me. Wisdom from others is a gift you can't put a price tag on. I must speak their names in such high regard throughout my journey, acknowledging their shining example of what it means to be a woman who will one day be known for her legacy. After being in a room with women who were intertwining their beautiful souls together, becoming even more of a powerful force totally rocked my world. I walked out taller with my head tilted higher, and I started dreaming bigger. That experience crowned me in ways I'll never be able to fully explain.

I love to see women rooting for one another, unafraid to share space with each other knowing it won't dim their light. I've witnessed women boldly speak others' names in rooms full of opportunities fit for them. Trust me, it will only make your light shine brighter when you display genuine kindness toward other queens. There will often be times when we will need each other. We must remind each other of the queen within us all when we stumble and fall. Extend a hand to help one another rise back up and stand even taller than before.

Straighten each other's crown when it is tilting. The path has been paved for you, so walk with your head high and chest out queen! Imagine if we all continue to celebrate and pay homage to those who came before us and stand next to us as we journey into the sisterhood of greatness and excellence. Just imagine that!

What queens have influenced you?

Day #13

CROWN ME QUEEN

AFFIRMATIONS

☞ I am a queen! I got this! When one of us wins we all win. I go hard for my sisters. I will give them deserving compliments and ensure them of their worth. Together we can accomplish anything we dream up.

☞ I am my sister's keeper. We survive to thrive and uplift one another. Today I will be living proof of God's goodness and favor. I will shine my light brighter than yesterday. I am strong, confident, resilient, and full of God's grace.

☞ My crown may tilt, but it will never fall off. My name is highly spoken in rooms I haven't even entered yet. God will make a seat at the table of excellence for me. I believe that God will provide a way for me to then set a table for my sisters of excellence to come join me.

☞ I am a goddess in the flesh. I walk with integrity and carry my pride better than any fashionable bag over my shoulder. I will not set limits on becoming all I can be. I have seen the queens who came before me break glass ceilings. I know the difference I can make in this world. I don't have to settle for anything less than God's promises for me.

☞ God was showing out when He made me. I am one of His best creations. I am uniquely made by His perfect hands. God said I am classic and will never go out of style. I will set my standards high and carry myself in a way that will make the next generation of women follow proud.

☞ God will place me in rooms that will blow my mind. I will plant seeds and reap the harvest that will allow me to bless others.

☞ I am soft, kind, strong, bold, brave, and clothed in dignity. I am beautiful not only on the outside but within because I practice being kind and speaking positivity. Even if I fall short, my sister will extend her hand to fix my crown because I am more than enough. We are more than enough. We are nurturers and the glue that holds this world together.

☞ The hand of God is in my life, therefore I always defeat the odds. I trust that God will continue to elevate me and continue to bless me with all the whispers I have prayed for.

Day #14

LET YOUR LIGHT SHINE

ONE THING I ONCE DESPISED about myself for a very long time was my kindness. Maybe that sounds a bit harsh, but it's true. I was wondering what was wrong with me that I just wanted to give and be a people-pleaser to everyone. I had a hard time saying "No" to things I didn't feel like doing. It was as if I had this fixation on being so darn nice and accommodating. My friends named me "the animal and human rescue lady," always wanting to help people or fix their situations. I was always giving out discounts instead of charging the full price even knowing I needed it, custom-making gifts for people just because only to look up and not feel the appreciation. Then I realized that was on me. I irritated myself because I had to learn the hard way that not everyone deserves my kindness. Nobody asked for anything, so why was I having these expectations? I always told my mother I blamed her because she's the same way. She cracks up laughing saying, "You'll learn who deserves your kindness and who doesn't in due time, my dear." I'd joke about wishing I didn't inherit that trait at times, more so because I hadn't learned who deserved my kindness or who to really distribute my generosity to.

There are a lot of people who will take advantage of your kindness if they are allowed to. Anyone who personally knows me will tell you that I'm a giver at heart. I'm so much like my mother it tickles me. I stock up on trinket gifts and celebratory cards so when occasions come around, I always have my gift goody bag to go to. Most of my friends or associates expect a gift with some shimmer to it from me. I love anything that shines. Bling and sparkle make me happy! Fine glitter is magical like angel dust! From the New York City streetlights and billboards to accessories around my wrist, there is something magical for me about things that glisten. I thoroughly enjoy gift-giving, even if it's from the Dollar Store. I love seeing someone smile and letting them know they were thought of. Anyone can give a gift or flowers, but I love the personal note or detailed touch that lets them know it's specifically about the thought of them. It's easy to let your light shine when you know you are appreciated. I was trying to figure out how to dim my light from takers and still shine at the same time. The key was simply to keep shining but to be in control of who deserves my light.

When you are a giver, whether it be of your time, money, love, etc., some people can tend to have expectations of you that can feel like pressure. I wasn't always comfortable using the word "No." I've witnessed people become very comfortable taking so much to the point where it becomes expected. Now I'm the "sorry, not sorry" girl. For a long time, I was uncomfortable enforcing my prices for my services. Entrepreneurs will quickly learn that your business will not thrive off freebies, and a special isn't special if you run it all the time. No one taught me how to be a business owner or a boss with boundaries. I always say selfish takers taught me. People know your worth, but they hope you don't. As an entrepreneur, it hurt me being "dumb kind" because kindness was not paying my bills. I was often being kind to the unappreciative folks and to the ones who could afford it. A lot of times, it's the ones who have it that want the discount. Nah, run me my money so I can pay my bills like you pay yours.

I quickly learned that as a giver, I must set limits because takers won't. The day I learned I could unapologetically be kind without shorting myself, my life changed. My light began to shine brighter, especially since my bills were getting paid. I realized I could be nice and still say "No" without dimming my light to appease others. Years ago, I remember a friend who would come to sit with me for chats and chuckles. She loved my dog Champ—RIP to the best furry friend there ever was. We would sometimes just sit in the kitchen and talk for hours. We would laugh, cry, share happy tears, sip wine, and laugh some more. She paused for a moment on this particular day and while sitting across from me said with a serious face, "Sandye, you have light around you." I said, "What do you mean?" I was thinking, "Girl, we are tipsy and that's a reflection off the window." She said, "You are the kind of person who can walk in a room and light it up. You have a way of making everyone feel special and seen, and that is a gift." She told me to never stay in a box and to always let my light shine. Tears rolled down my face. I was in a dark place at that time and honestly didn't think that my little mustard-seed size of light within was shining bright enough for anyone else to see. But those who carry light can see light even through the dark.

I have carried that with me to this day. One thing I can say is that I have been blessed with an amazing tribe who all like to see each other shine. We feed off each other's light. Sometimes being kind can be taken for a weakness. If your kindness has been taken for granted, remember it is the loss of others in the end because you gained the wisdom about who you should continue to share your light with. When you are a genuine giver, you don't do it to receive so when someone acknowledges your heart, it brings on an overwhelming ball of emotions filled with gratitude. I sometimes walk past my mirror with my brush singing, "Because I like what I see when I'm looking at me when I'm walking past the mirror." I learned to appreciate that beautiful trait I picked up from my mother.

Don't ever dim your light for anyone or anything! God is shining on you for you to shine on others. Do unto others as you'd want done to you. One of my good girlfriends would always say, "San, everyone is not like you, and you have to learn to accept that." Nowadays, I move with an open heart without expectations that can lead to disappointment. Some will assume if you're nice, you're less than smart. I always say don't ever get the two twisted because I always know what I am doing when I am giving of my love, finances, time, knowledge, etc. It is what I am choosing to do. Now if you burn that bridge, that is on you and will give me the insight on how I need to personally move forward with you. I will not, however, turn my light off or down and change who I am.

I'm not saying don't do a freebie or give out a discount or give in whatever way you choose to, but be wise about who you distribute your "gifts" to. I always say one kind act can save a life because we never know what someone else is going through. Random acts of kindness such as paying for the person's food or coffee in the drive through behind you may really make their day brighter than you will ever know. Keep your kind heart but be a smart "kind" of person. The world needs people like you. Always choose to let bitter situations make you better. Allowing someone else to block your light is giving them power that does not belong to them. Leave them in the shade and let your light shine brighter than ever!

How do you use your light? Do you remember a time when you'd hide your light to let someone else shine? Are you as kind to yourself as you are to others?

_____

_____

_____

_____

_____

_____

_____

_____

_____

_____

_____

_____

Day #14

LET YOUR LIGHT SHINE

AFFIRMATIONS

- My light will light the way for others. Today I will boldly walk in my light and allow it to shine bright.

- I am blessed to be a blessing. I am attentive and kind. I adjust to the rhythm of life and its ebbs and flows. Everywhere I go, I leave a trail of glitter. I am happy and feel ecstatic about all the good things coming my way today.

- I am an asset because of my giving spirit. Today I will attract nothing but positivity and blessings.

- I release the expectations I put on others to show up for me. I will always be true to who I am and expect nothing but the best for myself.

- I have good energy. I am dope. Those who understand the way I love are drawn to me. I am happy with the type of person I am. I will bet on myself today. I am so full of endless potential and creativity.

☞ Today I will do something that makes my spirit shine even brighter. God favors me and shines His light on me daily. I am a reflection of God's love for me. I won't leave any stone unturned while I live my life to the fullest.

☞ My light is going to draw in win after win. I'm on my way to reaching my full potential.

Day #15

MAINTAINING MY MENTAL

HAVE YOU EVER FELT as if you were losing it? Has your mind felt overwhelmed and cloudy, as if you were close to a breakdown if you didn't sit down and just be still? I have and it is not a good feeling. I've experienced feeling anxiety and dizziness as if the entire room is spinning out of control. Have you ever just felt mentally drained? If not, I hope you never do. I've learned to take a minute to think about what I'm feeding my mind daily. Sometimes you must tune out the noise surrounding you to protect your energy. That might be turning off the news, phone, social media, TV, radio, etc. Getting the proper sleep and rest is also a necessity to staying mentally alert and sane.

I always try to maintain being positive, but there are some

days when I rub myself the wrong way with negative thoughts that creep in my mind. At one point, life seemed to be ripping me to shreds. I found myself being the negative person I swore to never be. I began speaking negatively out loud. I call it the "Oh woe is me" mood. It's the constant complaining that this is going wrong, that is going wrong, underlining jokes about what is going wrong and that this isn't going right, blah, blah, blah. Complaining doesn't do anything to fix whatever it is. My girlfriend MC was what I call a real one. She noticed it and straight up checked me and made me aware of it. She started sending me positive videos to watch to help change my mind-set and how I viewed life events. When we would talk, if I even slanted my words toward a negative direction, she would redirect the tone of our conversations. She warned me to watch my tongue.

It was a raw reality check I needed and helped to shake me out of that bad habit I was developing. It took time, but it made me more conscious of how I was letting my mind go into a negative, dark place that led to those thoughts rolling off my tongue and spilling out onto others. I had to let worry, doubt and fears go. I had to speak life into my dead self. I had to take over my mental thoughts, look myself in the mirror, and speak positively to myself. I had to recite my affirmations daily and talk that talk. Not everything will always be easy breezy in life. Not everything will always have a great outcome. It's how we choose to react to life's situations. I was sending my blood pressure through the roof stressing about things that were out of my control. We must feed positive thoughts into our brain cells. This is why I love affirmations. Life can be mentally draining by itself, so find positive things to read and watch.

Go for walks to free your mind. Stretch your mind in a healthy place of thinking daily. Your morning thoughts can dictate the outcome of your day.

I also found that I had become cranky. I've struggled with insomnia for many years. The lack of sleep had me so off my A-game even though others may not have noticed because I was good at pushing through a day to another day to another day. I was irritable within, but still had to put on a smile even though I was so tired I could barely make my cheeks smile. I was always feeling drained, lethargic, and not performing at my best because my energy level was at "just get by." And yet, when I think of all I still accomplished, I can only imagine how much more I would have achieved had I not struggled with insomnia. I hadn't had a structured daily schedule, so my sleep pattern was always off. My eating habits were poor. I became programmed to hustle every hour that I could. I was hungry to survive and not fail, which meant no days off and the mindset that I'll sleep when I die mentality. Let me just tell you that I learned the hard way what burnout and not getting enough rest can do to you physically and mentally. Rest is needed to perform at our highest potential as humans.

Don't believe the hype of the hustle and no rest. I wish I would have learned a long time ago how to balance work, play, and life. Being a creative person, I feel like sometimes my brain never shuts off. When I lay down, no matter how tired I am, it's hard to fall asleep, especially through the whole night. I get more rest than sleep at times. My eyes may be closed, but I'm constantly thinking. I have worked on listening to soft music at night, not eating or drinking any liquids after a certain hour, and writing out my to-do list before bed so that I can take a load off of my mind. I envy people who can literally sleep through a whole night. I started paying more attention to what I listen to daily. I'm working on a consistent workout regimen. I try not to watch the news before going to bed.

How we absorb life daily affects us mentally. Are you listening to positive podcasts while driving? Maybe wind down with some soft music. I'm still working on meditation. I close my eyes, and my mind goes 100 miles a minute at times thinking of what I'm going to eat afterwards or errands I have to run. Training our thoughts can be challenging, but it is achievable. Turn off the computer and phone to wind down when needed because the light will keep you up. If you are like me, I can sometimes get caught on social media scrolling for new ideas that lead to one page to another page and another. Take a break from social media because it can drag you down a rabbit hole for hours if you let it. Again, I know this from experience.

With all that is going on in this crazy world, it is not easy to stay sane. Applaud yourself for how well you are doing because not everyone knows what it took for you to mentally show up for yourself, let alone others. Try recharging yourself as much as you do your phone. We cannot take being in our right mind for granted. We must nourish our brains just as we do our bodies. Prioritize your mental health.

What do you do to stay sane? How do you alleviate daily mental stress?

_____

_____

_____

_____

_____

_____

_____

_____

_____

_____

_____

_____

_____

_____

Day #15

MAINTAINING MY MENTAL

AFFIRMATIONS

☞ I love showing myself love and attention and mentally focusing on the good things happening around and for me. I am worth the effort I pour into myself.

☞ My self-care is necessary for my mental health. I am seeing the change I want to see one day at a time. I am so happy for myself.

☞ I know that I am doing the very best that I can. I am so proud of the progress I have made, seen and unseen.

☞ I feed my mind positive thoughts daily. I am in control of my thoughts. I can see the glow on me after I have nourished my mind and soul with positivity.

☞ I give myself permission to do what is best for me and my mental health. Today I will rest without feeling guilty. I will apologetically allow my mind to relax. I may spend time decluttering everything from my phone to home to keep my mind clear of clutter taking up unnecessary space, which can tend to cause mental confusion.

- My mind is sound. I have peace in my soul and my heart is full. I will maintain an attitude of gratitude daily.

- My thoughts hold the power in what I believe. I will think of nothing but good thoughts that soothe my spirit. My good thoughts will roll off of my tongue today and bless someone else.

- I am strong in my mind, body, and spirit. I can do hard things. I have beat the odds and done difficult things in the past. I will focus on finding solutions. I am capable of understanding mind over matter.

- My peace of mind is non negotiable.

Day #16

KNOW YOUR WORTH

DO YOU KNOW YOUR WORTH? Do you understand your value as a human being on this earth? As a young girl, I grew up wanting to be like my mother, aunts, and grandmother. I wasn't sure what that quite meant then, but my daily visual was our family bond. All I pretty much saw was motherhood without even understanding that. Our God-given gift as women is the ability to produce new life into this world. I thought that I would have four kids, just like my mom. My dad was adopted, so that made me want to adopt at some point. I have three older half-sisters, but I only know them as my whole sisters. I saw my big sisters being mothers and again looked forward to being a mom one day. Two of my brothers each have a daughter, and the love I've experienced being their auntie is deeper than any words.

After experiencing miscarriages, I started to question my

worth as a woman. I asked God, "Why am I broken? I am always good with other people's kids, so why am I not being blessed with my own?" Little did I know, I wasn't broken. It just wasn't for me to give birth. In my opinion, women are natural nurturers. I had a craving to do just that for my own children, but that was not what God had planned for me. When in my late 20s and 30s, doctors told me I was at a high-risk age. If I wanted to have children, I should get started asap. For most women, it truly makes you feel like your clock is ticking. You are in a race for time, a race to find the right partner if you don't have one. The race to be financially and physically ready to have a child can be overwhelming. I also had endured some not-so-nice experiences growing up, with rape being one of them. Some things I've chosen to take to my grave to maintain my own sanity. I never talked about this much in detail because it's still a way of shielding myself. I will say the damage it did mentally made me question if I would be able to be a good mother because I felt I may always fear not being able to protect my child/children from the gross beings in this world. Yet my stronger thoughts were that I am a woman. I have seen the strength of a woman who carried the same baggage of thoughts and are excellent mothers, so I was willing to try.

It seems like every relationship I had been in, my significant other had already experienced having a child or children. When someone has already had a certain experience, they aren't always eager to check that off their list of things to do or accomplish as you are. Eventually I started to accept that having children was not meant to be a part of my journey or something I was supposed to experience, so I needed to stop questioning God and be happy that I have other people's kids to love on, add humor, and send home. It's funny how time can be a gift and a curse. I started out thinking one way but in the end, I had to find peace with my reality. I try my best to seek and trust God's timing and not my own. At this point in my life, my goal is for my needs, wants, and desires to align with God's blueprint and purpose for my life. I share this because I know so many women who experience riding that rollercoaster of thoughts. Technology is so different these days because women are now having children in their mid 40s and up. There is more information about freezing eggs and other options. It was a hard pill to swallow at times, but I am now completely at peace knowing that I am not having children at this point in my life, and that does not define my worth as a woman. I get to love everyone else's children wholeheartedly and that fulfills me!

Hold on to your seats and grab a fan y'all!! I'm about to get really REAL!! This is for women who have experienced what I'm about to share or will experience it in their future: Menopause! Lawwwwd!!! Talk about an emotionally hormonal ride through the fire pits of hell that I didn't see coming. I can laugh now but trust me, it's no laughing matter when you are experiencing an internal hot flash; gaining weight; experiencing memory loss, fatigue, body aches; and losing hair, among other symptoms. The first time I experienced someone having a hot flash, I was working with a client and sweat started boiling on her forehead and nose like heat rising off a hot pavement after a downpour of rain. When she sat upward, I noticed she had her dress on inside out. She and I laugh about it now. She called it a meltdown rather than a hot flash because that's how discombobulated it can have you. She said, "Honey, I'm gonna need that fan!" I politely handed it to her without asking any questions except for if she needed some water. Then I experienced my girlfriends pulling out small, hand-held fans at dinner, and so forth. Women started asking me if I was selling the fans I used at work. I was blown away at how common this was because it wasn't something I had heard talked about often, yet I had worked primarily with women.

When you hit your late 40s and 50s, it is a topic that most women learn about quickly because for most, we don't have a choice. I thought the late-night sweats were because I like spicy foods or just a chemical imbalance but what do you know. There I was receiving a fan shaped like a cute perfume bottle from my girlfriend as I joined the club. Now I'm the woman with handheld fans in my nightstand top drawer, car, and purse next to my 10 pairs of reader glasses. Father Time is real! Listen, as women we so need to have these discussions. Here was my deal: I have two, very small fibroids that haven't been an issue for years. One evening, I was standing in my closest changing clothes. I felt something drop out of me. The clots continued throughout the night. I had no idea what was happening, but it scared me to death. I really thought it was my "Come to Jesus" moment. I ended up in the emergency room wondering why I was severely hemorrhaging. I was in the ER texting my mom and aunts on a group chat giving them my symptoms and asking for prayers. The doctors thought they would have to give me a blood transfusion at one point, but my body was reproducing almost as quickly as I was losing from what they said. I literally thought I was dying from the inside out and was trying to mentally prepare myself to be strong for whatever the results would be. After several tests, I found out

I was going through perimenopause. Excuse me doc, say what now!?!

One of my aunts then told me about her similar experience, another told me about having endometriosis, and another shared her experience when going into menopause. My mother said she had never experienced hot flashes or anything like what I went through. I thought, "Now why didn't I get that gene passed down to me from her?" Everything else is just like my mom, from my hands to ankles. She literally falls out laughing every time I say that to her when I'm having a hot summer moment, which is what she calls it. The thing that got me the most was that this was never discussed until I started experiencing it. It would have saved me a lot of mental torture had I been aware of these types of symptoms, which is why I am sharing this.

Once the scene was clear, if you know what I mean, there was a fibroid found in the cavity of my uterus lining that I ended up having removed. I was due to go back to Maryland to have some important things done with my mom that we'd put in place after she was diagnosed with congestive heart failure months prior, but I had to cancel last minute. This was a scary time we shared as mother and daughter, and it brought us extra close as women. It has made our conversations about any and everything heighten. When the doctor mentioned a possible hysterectomy, I felt a brick hit my chest and the tears flowed. I had already come to grips with making the decision of not having kids, but it was different hearing someone say they may have to take that option away from me if I wanted to change my mind. Going through this experience opened up a can of worms, as they say. I had to get a biopsy done to make sure there wasn't any cancer. I thank God for the negative result, and I didn't have to get a hysterectomy after getting a second doctor's opinion.

Once I spoke about my experience openly to others, I started to hear more and more stories similar to mine. Now it's like Pandora's Box is open. It's all I hear about at my age, but I am so glad it is being talked about on many public platforms now. I've had to slack off my glass of red wine at night because I tend to become a whole overheated sweatbox that wants to just stand in the front of the freezer naked with the door open. I was feeling a deep darkness daily, and I couldn't pull myself out of it because I didn't know what it was. I didn't feel like myself at all, but I couldn't pinpoint what was going on. It literally crippled me physically at one point. I was slowly walking around my bedroom holding onto my bedpost and dresser trying to stand while crying out to God to make whatever was happening stop. I was an emotional trainwreck for what felt like eternity. I didn't feel like doing my hair or putting on anything other than pj's and any lightweight material. I could cry at the drop of a dime for no reason. I could be in the grocery store line and just want to weep. My hormones were all over the place.

Things are better since I had the myomectomy procedure to remove that fibroid, but it's still touch and go at times. If I snap, forgive me because my patience is not like it was in my 20s. I wanted to touch on this because it needs to be an open dialogue for women. I don't want to scare anyone, but I do want to educate. Everyone's body and symptoms are different. I feel that if I had the knowledge about this, it wouldn't have caught me so off guard.

When I was younger, I learned that my dad was adopted. I told myself I would consider adopting because of that. I saw firsthand how love can change a person's life and have a ripple effect on us all to make the world a better place. One of my girlfriend's adopted and the way she loves that child to the ends of this earth fills my heart up to witness. Her love falls nothing short of a mother's love. A woman's worth is not based on if we bare children but how we love and pour into them. God's plan and not my own. I understand now that God wasn't asking me to figure out that part of my life. He's asking me to trust that He already has. I love being Auntie San and to be honest, I love that God has provided me the opportunity to be a bonus mom. Now that I know what I know as it relates to where I am in my life, I wouldn't change it because I know my worth as a loving woman.

What's one situation in life that helped you understand your worth is not less than?

_____

_____

_____

_____

_____

_____

_____

_____

_____

_____

_____

_____

_____

Day #16

KNOW YOUR WORTH

AFFIRMATIONS

- I am a nurturer by nature. I owe it to myself to always show up for me first. I am worthy of everything I can dream up for myself.

- I am the author of my own story. I will write it in ways that celebrate all that I am and strive to be. Someone will relate to how worthy they are through me sharing my testimonies therefore, I will continue to heal out loud because I almost died silently. I am aligned with my purpose of knowing my worth and helping others to know theirs.

- I am divinely made to give and receive love. I am more than enough. I am worthy of respect and the best. I will not chase or settle. I will love others the way I want to be loved.

- I am open to receiving compliments. I'm flawed and beautifully made. I will share my wisdom gained through challenges so someone knows they are not alone.

- I am worthy no matter what cards I am dealt. I am fully committed to focusing on building my own personal growth and development. I believe in myself and all that God has called me to be.

- God put me together perfectly and will always lead me to the path that was created for me.

- My self-worth is not defined by others' opinions. The love I give will make its way back to me and my story will inspire others.

- My worth is not debatable. I am intentional with the love I give to others.

- I am worthy of a life filled with peace, purpose, and prosperity.

Day #17

PUSH THROUGH

HOW MANY TIMES have you wanted to throw in the towel? Life can really be a lot, especially if you are living it. Reread that. If you are really living life, then life is going to happen. Deep, right? Or not so much? Troubles, worries, and stress will appear throughout your lifetime. Some things can't be avoided and have to be faced head-on in order to get through and over to the other side. You can find yourself stuck and paralyzed at times. Other times I know I have felt frustrated as if I was on a hamster wheel running nonstop. Let's be honest, neither is a good feeling. Staying stuck can feel as if quicksand is slowly taking you under into suffocation. Life can hit you with some blows that put you in pockets of depression. I'm learning when life throws a punch to throw a punch back. There were times when I would express how I just wanted to go sit up on a cloud for a few days away from it all and come back down to reality later.

One thing about me is that I'm never afraid to push through and start over if I must. But just like most, I don't like the yucky feeling while pushing through. So many times I have wanted to quit but I just can't, and even that has been frustrating. I wonder how many people reading this have had that feeling. I've learned to appreciate the chances and strength God gives us to try and try again. Tough situations don't always last, but enough people do. I know that even if I'm feeling weak, I am still tough. I can feel both strong and weak at the same time. Some folks are afraid of trying something new. I feel as if I'm on my fourth life. They say life is 90% what happens to you and 10% how you respond to it. I have survived my hardest days in life so far, so I have found that to be close to true for me.

My youngest brother has epilepsy. He started having seizures when he was around 6 or 7 years old. He now has grand mal seizures in his mid 40s, but he is forever my baby brother. He has never been able to live a normal life—drive a car, work, travel on a plane, etc. But he has never given up on life. He continues to push through and is one of the strongest people I know. He falls but always gets back up each time and tries to live the life he didn't choose as best he can. It is mentally excruciating to watch a loved one go through that kind of experience. It can make you feel helpless, but my baby brother has made me rethink the way I look at his situation and duo diagnosis. I started thinking about how I get the privilege to choose the life I want daily. With all he has endured–from blow to blow to his head on solid concrete to stitches, to staples, to numerous needles–he is living proof that God has us all here for a reason. Whatever you are going through, keep picking yourself up and pushing forward. You never know who is being inspired by your will to not give up. My baby brother is one of my biggest inspirations. His tenacity gives me the courage to push through unforeseen obstacles and to know that things could always be worse. Even when you don't have all the answers, keep pushing forward. I hope we all strive to push past our circumstances and try to make the best life we can for ourselves with the hand we're dealt.

What's one obstacle you recall having to push through even when you felt weak?

_____

_____

_____

_____

_____

_____

_____

_____

_____

_____

_____

_____

_____

Day #17

PUSH THROUGH

AFFIRMATIONS

- I wake up every day with the will to live my best life. I am focused, and I am a finisher.

- All my dreams are on the other side of my comfort zone. I give myself permission to dream and believe again and again.

- I will always maximize my potential and push through all obstacles to reach my destined success.

- I am making progress even if it's slow baby steps. I am constantly evolving and growing.

- Anything from my past will never hold me back because I am excited about my future.

- I am capable of handling whatever comes my way. Being able to push through tough situations has been my superpower.

- My circumstances don't define me. Blessings will always come my way because I lead with good intentions.

- I will always get back up from a fall because God extends his hand out to me daily. I turn my setbacks into stepping stones. I will shatter glass and kick doors open. Nothing can stop me. I will always push through whatever may be trying to stop or slow me down.

Day #18

PURPOSE & PASSION

A RE YOU THE TYPE OF PERSON to look at every ending as a new beginning? The day I watched my grandmother, affectionately called Mum, take her last breath due to cancer, a big piece of me died in that moment. She had become my protector in many ways after my dad passed. She was there for me on every level. My grandmother was a wise God-fearing woman. She was strong, yet gentle. She was the family glue that held us together, the queen of the family who didn't take NO stuff. She gave that kick-hug kind of love. She was very stern yet warmhearted, poised, and well-spoken. She could give you a look that could break you down and build you back up in the same moment if you did something out of line.

My grandmother owned a clothing store in the neighborhood where I grew up as a child. She named it Michele after my aunt, her youngest daughter. As much as I was a tomboy at a young age, I would often play dress-up in my aunt's clothes. I would stand in her shoes to be taller. My other grandmother who adopted my dad worked in a hair salon in the same shopping center area. Maybe that's where I got the combination of entrepreneurship in the beauty and fashion industry. When I got older and my Mum fell ill to cancer, I would brush her hair as it was thinning, file her fingernails, and put lipstick on her. I just remember how grooming her seemed to make her feel better. I still remember her smile and what her hands felt like. Being the first blood granddaughter, I was very close to Mum. After she passed away, I lived lost in New Jersey figuring out what my career choice was going to be. I had my disability and medical knowledge from my previous work position, and I'd always loved being a part of the beauty and fashion industry. I knew I enjoyed helping people by making them feel and look good. It was then I had that "aha" moment! It dawned on me that I am a purposeful person. How do I combine my passions into my life's purpose?

There is no one purpose for me to tap into, there are many. I decided to get my cosmetology license, something that no one could ever take from me. I could use those skills anywhere in the world. It was more than just learning about how to style hair or do a facial. I enjoyed learning about the layers of the skin, the anatomy of the eye, skin diseases, and hair growth cycles. I was also certified as an eyelash extension technician. I wanted to help cancer survivors nurse their hair and lashes back to a healthy state. Enhancing beauty was such a rewarding feeling for me to see how it would spruce up someone's spirit. It always reminded me of my grandmother and having a purpose. When we look good, we feel good! Losing my grandmother was a death that came with a rebirth for me, a chance to honor her and make her proud. She is my very own angel who led me to one of my purposes. Sometimes it is not about the dollar if what you are pouring into others is priceless. I found that my purpose and passion most times lead to profit. The money will come when you love what you do and put in the work. As an entrepreneur, this is how I reinvent myself when it is time to move into a new career chapter. Passion, purpose, project. Whether it be a friendship, relationship, etc., I view it as a new beginning more so than focus on the ending.

I remember a very popular DJ known worldwide posting on social media about his journey relating to resilience and reinventing himself several times. I admire the fact that throughout his journey, he stayed true to himself and remained humble. He's one of the coolest and genuinely nicest humans I know. He is living successfully using his God-given gifts. He unselfishly shared one of his gifts with the world to heal it in its darkest time: Music! Music is a universal magnet that draws people of all ethnicities together, doesn't matter rich, poor, disabled, etc. Music can be healing. Talk about using your gift to bless others—purpose and passion at its greatest led by example. To see people find that thing that ignites their fire is admirable. To make a living while doing what you love is a double blessing. Sometimes how you view new beginnings is all in your mindset. Granted we all must make a living, so I'm all for finding your passion in hopes it will lead to your purpose and peace, and that both will lead to a paycheck. Throughout our life journey, our passions may change, but I encourage you to always find purpose in what you are doing. It is the way to self-fulfillment.

What are you passionate about? Has it helped you find a piece of your purpose?

_____

_____

_____

_____

_____

_____

_____

_____

_____

_____

_____

_____

Day #18

PASSION & PURPOSE

AFFIRMATIONS

- I see every ending as a new beginning. I am passionate about my future and the things that I deserve and love.

- I live a purposeful life. I am a multi-purposeful person. I keep people around me who don't hesitate to support and encourage me.

- I will use all the gifts and talents God has given me to make a difference in this world. I am significant and confident about my purpose in life.

- I'm a dreamer, a natural-born visionary. I am allowed to live many lives in this lifetime. I will venture into new careers as I continue to find new passions that ignite my life's purpose.

- God knew what He was doing when I was created. I was born with purpose.

☞ My passion drives me beyond my wildest imagination. I am manifesting everything I can dream up. I am extremely passionate about doing God's work and living a meaningful life.

☞ I run ahead where there is no path because I am confident in where I'll end up. Knowing my purpose leads me to great possibilities.

☞ I am passionate about my life's purpose. I will leave a legacy that has been impactful on this world.

Day #19
TAKE THE RISK

RE YOU the "shoulda, coulda, woulda" person? Are you spontaneous? Adventurous or a risk-taker? Do you consider yourself brave? Are you afraid of failure? My mom always says nothing beats a failure more than someone who tries. Do you vicariously live through others because it feels safer? I always tell myself to leap and take a risk by at least trying. No risk, no reward. If you don't take the risk, you miss the opportunity. I feel as if the way my life was set up forced me to be a risk-taker, however, I was not always in tune with understanding that. I used to worry about what people might say if I didn't succeed in whatever new thing I decided to try. I would worry myself to no end thinking about what if something doesn't work out. Do I have a Plan B lined up just in case Plan A doesn't work out? Then I got to a point where I stopped caring about what others might say. I felt so free once I got to that point. I have taken many risks, including writing this book. If we live with the mindset of YOLO, then why not try all the things that interest you?

Speaking of interests, I took an interest in acting. I put in all the background work and hours from shows such as *Law and Order* and *The Red and Method Man Show* to movies such as *The Beauty Shop* to become a SAG member. I took acting classes with some of the best coaches to try to hone in on the craft. I remember the opportunity to audition for a part on a TV series being filmed in Atlanta. I repeatedly studied my lines and had them confidently down. You couldn't tell me nothing! I was so extra confident when I walked into the audition, I just knew I would nail it. As soon as I got in front of the camera and casting director, I totally froze. My mind went blank. The more I tried not to over think, I was overthinking so much I couldn't think straight. I felt like such a failure at that moment. The more I tried to remember my lines and get into character, the harder it was because my nervousness took over. I realized that my memory wasn't the best when it came to remembering lines pressed up against my nerves. I found that I was more comfortable freely improvising, hosting, interviewing, and being a part of speaking panels. As embarrassed as I felt at that moment, I was so proud that I had given it a shot. I mean hey, what if my nerves hadn't paralyzed my mind? I might have been the next Viola Davis. Laugh if you will but seriously, that is what life is about—trying new things that interest you because you never know where it may lead you to or what you might be good at.

Are you ready to take the risk if someone is willing to take a risk on you? Have you prepared for the things you want and asked God for in prayer? I have a girlfriend who is a highly respected boss chick making major moves in what was once considered a male-dominated industry. I say once in past tense because she and her COO are a dynamic duo turning the tables and changing the game in their industry. I hold them in such high regard and look up to them both personally and professionally. From sneakers to heels, my friend is one of the smartest, savviest, kindhearted humans on this planet. But don't get it twisted because she is most definitely about handling business. I love her like a sister and admire her work ethic and poise. She's really just a dope person. I'm always taking notes from the sideline. Now you will understand why what I'm about to share was such a big deal for me.

We were having lunch one day and she surprisingly offered me the opportunity to set up my beauty business in a really amazing location she had in Atlanta because it had been sitting dormant for a while. I was completely flabbergasted! It was like a dream come true, and I was in awe that she thought so highly of me from a business standpoint to even consider giving me that opportunity. I laid in bed that night for hours staring at the ceiling thanking God for that opportunity. I immediately started thinking of ways to make this the most creative and successful opportunity ever. I thought making it a beauty and wellness business center would be ideal because there weren't any like it in the nearby and surrounding areas. After doing much research, I realized it was a desire that the local community wanted to have. I kept open my old location, which was the size of one room compared to a three-story space. I was scared as hell but expeditiously jumped into bringing my vision to life at the new location. I literally made about six trips back and forth with my vehicle alone loaded up to the top with equipment to take to the location, from massage tables and a nail station to yoga matts, makeup chairs, desks and bookshelves. I had contractors come to discuss where TVs would hang and a yoga and fitness instructor ready to start teaching classes once everything was ready. I was over the moon excited and terrified at the same time, but I was going to do whatever it took not to let my friend or myself down.

The opportunity ended up having to take a shift for another business opportunity, but my point in sharing is I was ready to jump in and go, scared and all. I surprised myself by not letting fear of the unknown stop me from being willing to try something new on such a large scale. Sometimes taking a leap leaves no time to sit in fear. I learned to just go, move, take a step. Just don't get stuck standing still. Sometimes all it takes is just for one person to believe in you, but you must believe in yourself from the start. When people take a chance on you and they don't have to, that speaks volumes about how they view you, your character, and your work ethic. The thought that she was even willing to give me that opportunity opened my eyes to continue to dream big and to stay ready for any opportunities I pray for that might come my way. I will forever be beyond grateful for the love and support my friend has poured into me since the day we met.

Have you ever slowed down and tried something new outside of your norm? During the pandemic, I went out on a limb since I finally had some much-needed downtime and decided to try things I normally didn't get to do when I was working full time. My new creative hobby was making beautiful home decor and art using resin. To be honest, I had never heard of resin before this endeavor. I always loved painting on canvases and trying DIY projects but playing with chemicals wasn't on my list, especially having gone through lung issues. I taught myself through trial and error. I fell back in love with the freedom to create. Creating has no boundaries or limits. There I was with another venture under my belt, doing something that I enjoyed in my free time that led to profit. I share this because people will sometimes only see you through their tunnel vision. They may put limits on what they think you can and can't do. Screw that. I can't stress this enough: If you are on the edge of uncertainty, don't be afraid to believe in yourself. Explore all your possibilities and tap into all your potential. That's when you stumble across what you may like or be good at. If I have learned anything, it is to just jump out there and take risks.

Sometimes your closest friends or family may not understand what your vision, goal, or dream is. That's ok. God put it in you, not them. To top it off, they may not mean any harm if they show signs of disbelief or voice an opinion that could discourage you. Either way, your life's assignments are for you to fulfill and not anyone else. That's what makes you uniquely you. You may not always get the support you'd want, but that's ok also. Cue in Alexa to play "Encourage Yourself!" Do the things that move your soul and get you excited! I'm not here to live a mediocre life. I'm here to take the risk of living the best and most dynamic life I can create filled with my passion and purpose. I will not be placed in a box. Will you?

I once told a friend I was going out on a ledge and taking risks. My friend said, "What if you fall?" I said, "But what if I FLY?" What is one risk you'd like to take or should have taken? What is something new that you'd like to try? When you get the opportunity to shoot your shot, will you take it?

_____

_____

_____

_____

_____

_____

_____

_____

_____

_____

_____

Day #19

TAKE THE RISK

AFFIRMATIONS

- ☞ I wasn't born to be average, so I will take the risk of believing anything is possible for me. Taking a risk is better than feeling regret.

- ☞ I without a doubt believe that I am deserving of my dreams and desires. Today blessings and unforeseen opportunities will fall in my lap.

- ☞ I am not afraid of taking risks. I am confident in myself. I am courageous and will leap beyond my comfort zone because I deserve a life full of all the things that make me happy.

- ☞ My life is full of adventures and spontaneity. Today I choose to step out on faith. Today I will try something new.

- ☞ God has been preparing me for greater things. His love for me has superseded anything I could imagine. I am not afraid to reach for the stars and beyond.

☞ Every day is full of potential opportunities. I will take the risk to reap the reward.

☞ I'm aiming for the moon and the stars. My life is fun and fruitful. I'm constantly creating new memories by trying new things.

☞ I'm open to new ideas and concepts. I will never put limits on myself. I'm willing to ask for help if needed. Asking for help is courageous. It is not a form of weakness if I am putting forth my own effort.

☞ I can do anything I put my mind to. God is about to finance the vision He put inside of me. It's only up from here, and I'm ready.

☞ I'm a magnet for wealth, joy, peace, prosperity, and unexpected blessings. I will leap into the unknown of God's promises without hesitation.

Day #20

FOCUSED & FEARLESS

I SOMETIMES HAVE the most difficult time staying focused on one thing at a time. I wonder how many can relate to what I'm about to say. Heck, it took me forever to get this book done. I had to learn my style of writing. Some days I needed it to be a completely quiet environment alone to focus and other days or hours I needed soft music in the background so my mind wouldn't wander too far off of what I needed to be focused on while writing. I have so many things going on in my head at once that it's sometimes beyond challenging to not be all over the place trying to accomplish everything at once. If you sat in a corner watching me move and tried to figure out what I'm doing, I would have your head messed up and on a swivel. I have developed a fearless attitude of thinking I can accomplish anything and everything. The problem is while that is an ambitious way of thinking, I have had to learn to focus on one task at a time. For example, I literally will be all over my house starting one task and jumping into another before finishing what I started. I may start purging clothes and take them to a container in the garage, which will lead to me organizing the garage before heading to the kitchen to grab water, which leads to putting dishes away to going to the bathroom. I come out and see my computer, hop on to finish something I was working on only to have my mind wandering off about a creative project I can work on, which leads me to my craft room to something else to something else to something else. You see what I just did there?!

Some call it multi-tasking, but I call it being all over the place. Maybe it's ADD. In order for me to stay focused on a particular task at hand, I have to consistently practice self-discipline. I must get in and out of my own head. I must keep a structured schedule. I put everything on my calendar, from a leisure day to a business day. I can easily start little fires every-where within minutes, especially as a creative being. My mind tends to wander quickly into what I could or should be doing next. I guess I'm considered old school because I also like to write everything down. I put notes in my phone, stickies on my mirror, and I still have notepads to journal and jot down all my ideas. I'm a visual person and need to see my thoughts. Whatever it takes for me to stay organized I do because it helps to keep me focused. Even if I write a "to-do list" for the day, I can end up doing five other things that weren't on the list. It's not to say I always stay on course, but I try.

156

I often must ask myself, "What's on the other side of fear?" Do your goals scare you? Are you fearlessly doing you? I remember being in St. Barth's a very long time ago having breakfast with a very smart businesswoman and model I was cool with back when. I was older than she was, but she was far wiser than I was at her age. She was a real fashionista who chose to live life on her terms and always carried herself in a poised manner that displayed unshakeable confidence. I would overhear her business calls and watch how she ran her brand with a humble spirit but never settling for less than wanted and expected, which gained her so much respect. She was super business savvy and a well-spoken world traveler. Talk about boss, bold, beauty, brains, and business! She had it all wrapped up in one. Her beauty was effortless, and she was always full of good energy and sound advice. I learned so much from just watching her fearlessly be her authentic self unapologetically.

I'm always in admiration of women who fearlessly walk their walk and talk their talk without stepping on others. They pick a goal and smash it, reaching back to pull someone else up, never afraid that it will take away from them. The aroma of confidence is in the air when they are in the same room. I feed off that kind of energy. Manifestation is about believing and becoming. There is no room for fear when you are trying to focus on God's promises for you. As my confidence grew, I learned to do things even when scared. I walk into a room like God sent me, feeling sure of myself commanding the same energy that I exude. It took trying something one time and failing at it to not fear trying it again. I stopped caring about other people's opinions a long time ago. Caring about what others think will stifle progress. You can put being fearless in the category of taking risks. Once I learned I could bounce back and try again, it truly made me develop a fearless mindset.

When you fail at trying something new, will it fold or mold you? You make the choice. Insecurities and doubt will try to creep in, the mind will play tricks on you and obstacles will surface, but you must be fearless enough to tackle them while shaking in your boots. Being fearless comes with a level of confidence that will make those around you want to vibe higher and level up a notch. It may also make some uncomfortable. Those are not your people but always remember, people are watching even though they pretend not to be. You never know who you're inspiring, so keep pressing on and pushing through. Surround yourself with people who are focused on consistently growing, drinking their water, and minding their business. Dreamers, doers, and fearless faith-walkers with unstoppable energy are contagious, if you ask me.

What's one thing you need to fearlessly focus on? Who has had an influence on you becoming more fearless?

_____

_____

_____

_____

_____

_____

_____

_____

_____

_____

_____

_____

_____

_____

Day #20

FOCUSED & FEARLESS

AFFIRMATIONS

- ☞ I am focused on what I can control and fearlessly going after everything I want. I lead my life with determination. I am unstoppable and unbreakable.

- ☞ My will to succeed and become the best version of myself is my way of thanking the creator for this opportunity called life.

- ☞ Fear is an illusion that appears real. I will not succumb to fear. I am fearless, focused, and a force to be reckoned with. I will give myself permission to take up space and soar beyond my wildest imagination .

- ☞ I push past anxiety and my fears to reach a higher form of peace. I will face all uncertainty with confidence and courage. Fear won't stop me from reaching my full potential.

- ☞ There is power in my tongue. I won't be afraid to speak my mind and fiercely walk in the direction God is leading. It's always going to be peace over perfection and faith over fear.

- Today will be full of abundance because I woke up with a winning attitude.

- If I stay focused on what God has for me, I will always win! I fear not because my possibilities are endless with God by my side.

- I am surrounded by so much love and support that I need not fear. I am never alone. I am focused on flourishing, and I can see the footprints in the sand. I'm entering one of the best seasons of my life.

- I prayed for this life I am living today. My faith is bigger than any fear I may have. I am confident in who I am.

- I will be fiercer, finer, wiser, healthier, wealthier, and happier than I was yesterday and the day before that.

Day #21

LIVING LIFE INTENTIONALLY

*I*CAME UP DURING an era where "going hard in the paint" was glorified. I still have those times when I feel as if I'm running myself in the ground, and I must catch myself. I understand the new popular saying, "I want a soft life."

Have you ever felt as if you didn't have control of your life or your time? Your energy? For years I felt as if life was dragging me and I wasn't fully in control of living it the way I wanted to. I wasn't intentional with my daily routine, how my time was spent consistently, or who it was spent with. I was so busy working to build my brand for stability that I wasn't carving out time to take a lunch break or eat healthy. My hustle literally felt like four hours of inconsistent sleep, if that, and then back at it. These things matter as it relates to accomplishing your goals and the height of your success, but we must give ourselves grace in finding balance. We must intentionally find time to heal in areas where we are broken to live a full life with peace. We must be intentional about allowing our bodies and minds to rest so they can perform at their best. Be intentional about spending time with the ones we love and those who love us. Create better eating habits and work out.

I'm on a group chat with some of my female friends from Baltimore. At the beginning of every year, we are supposed to share our personal "intent" word or words in terms of our expectations for self. I love this because it makes you feel held accountable to achieve those goals. It's that little shove to keep you being intentional about what is important to you. I intentionally plan out vacations and check off my bucket list of new things to do, places to explore near and far. I jot in my notes what foods I want to try. Sometimes I just go to the park and people watch. Trust me, that's the best free show on earth. I'm more intentional about my spiritual growth. I believe you only get one life on this earth, but every day is a new day of living if you look at it that way. So why not live it to the fullest and be intentional about it? I felt I had cheated death many times, walking away from awful car accidents and all. One accident, the car flipped multiple times on a highway landing upside down, resulting in serious health issues. God spared me to give me the opportunity to live more intentionally. Have you ever felt that way?

That is why I wanted to share pieces of me and my journey with you. If you haven't started to live intentionally, now is the time. I have more trails of glitter to leave behind. Do all the things your heart desires. I wanted to try modeling and landed my face on a Dark and Lovely box internationally, the cover of Jamaica's *Fashion Week* local newspaper, walked the runway for the infamous Paul Mitchell, and so on. I wanted to try acting, so I pursued it and became a member in the union. I wanted to write a book and Walaa!! I'm proud of all that I have tried and all that I have accomplished. Pick one goal at a time and focus on it, but don't let that be it if you want to try other things. Knowing that I put the work in and nothing was just given to me fuels me to reach higher. I thank God for anyone who extended a hand throughout my journey or spoke my name in favor.

My creative juices are flowing at an all-time high, so who knows what's next for me. The sky isn't even the limit as far as I can see. I still have a long way to go! When you live a life full of intentions, you truly start to become who you are meant to be. I intentionally tell people I love them. It's not a slip-up. I mean what I say because I don't want to live with regret. I am not wasting anymore time now that I know what I want and have to offer. I make time to reflect on all God has done for me. He has been so good to me. My prayers are specific and intentional. Intentionally seek out your purpose and shoot your shot. Indulge in hobbies that bring you joy. Hang with people who make you happy and bring out the best in you. Don't put limits on how you love, but do love smart. And don't forget to tend to your self-care. Become more intentional about loving your body and what you put in it. That temple is your first home and a gift from God. If that crumbles, then what?

Intentionally make time for friends and family, and nourish those relationships. Remove those who disturb your peace, whether friends or family. Don't live to work just to be able to pay bills. Make a living, but don't neglect making a life. Create a balance that offers you time to enjoy life. We only live once but if you think off the grid, we only die once. Every day that we wake up we get to live anew. Explore and find new adventures. This second half of my life, I am intentionally going all out unapologetically and leaving no crumbs on the table. Life is to be lived! I am going to absorb it all and leave trails of glitter everywhere. If you look for me, I won't be hard to find. I'll be out here intentionally living, learning, and loving smart!

Are you intentionally living your best life? What are some things you will do to start living each day to its fullest?

_____

_____

_____

_____

_____

_____

_____

_____

_____

_____

_____

_____

_____

Day #21

LIVING LIFE INTENTIONALLY

AFFIRMATIONS

- I am intentional with how I choose to live my life from day to day. I will live life on my terms. I make my own rules and choose happiness daily.

- My Intentions are for the good of my future. I intentionally move in the direction of progression. I intentionally make room for growth and love.

- I will crush my goals and exceed my own expectations. I won't focus on perfection more than I will on achieving my goal. Everything will not always go according to plan, but I will always appreciate the effort I put forth and expect to succeed.

- My decisions are intentionally based upon what is best for me.

- I go the extra mile to make sure I am living my best life and am genuinely happy.

- ☞ I'm expecting good things to happen for me and those I love.

- ☞ I will live my best life while living. I will live each day as if it is my last. I will intentionally be brave enough to run over my fears and tackle any obstacle that stands in my way of the life I want and deserve.

- ☞ Today I am grateful for another day of life. I won't leave my life to chance. I have a new level of expectations for the life I want, and it includes love, peace, prosperity, new experiences, and adventures.

- ☞ I love life, so life loves me back.

About The Author

 ANDRIA LOMAX known as Sandye is a well respected name in the world of beauty, artistry, entertainment and fashion. Her entrepreneurial spirit is a force to be reckoned with. She has created a lifestyle brand that encompasses all the things she loves and enjoys. As a creative she will not set limits on building her brand. Sandye began her career in the fashion industry as a teen model while working for the State of Maryland for over fifteen years departing as a Disability Specialist to pursue her dreams of combining her passions with her God given talents. She wholeheartedly believes true beauty starts within and enhancing beauty by making people feel and look good has been a blessing for her. Choosing to work closely with cancer survivors in honor of her late grandmother has been a double blessing. Most might say she is a triple threat in the beauty business alone. Sandye is a licensed Cosmetologist, Esthetician and certified Makeup Artist. You've seen her work on major tv networks, Nike ads, some of your favorite celebrities and on movie screens. Sandye has also indulged in front of the camera modeling for brands like L'Oreal, Dark and Lovely and Paul Mitchell to name a few. Sandye is very passionate about sharing the awareness of epilepsy and cancer. Now she is adding becoming an author to her list of achievements. As a dedicated philanthropist, Sandye continues to use her platform to uplift and inspire women globally by sharing her life's journey and testimonies.

Visit her online at:
SandyeLomax.com;
Instagram and Facebook @SandyeLomax;
LinkedIn and Linktree;
beautyfetishbizz@gmail.com

"For I know the plans I have for you," declares the Lord. "Plans to prosper you and not to harm you, plans to give you hope and a future."

Jeremiah 29:11

www.ingramcontent.com/pod-product-compliance
Lightning Source LLC
Chambersburg PA
CBHW061754120626
46550CB00005B/1991